T0271103

Responsible Citizens and Sustainable Consumer Behavior

There is broad consensus on the need to shift to a new paradigm of lifestyles and economic development, given the unsustainability of current patterns. Research on consumer behavior is to play a crucial role in shedding light on the motives underpinning the adoption of responsible behaviors.

Stemming from a thorough discussion of existing approaches, this book argues that the perspective of analysis has to be modified. First, acknowledging that a profile of the responsible consumer does not exist, since all of us can be more or less sustainable and environment-friendly: the sustainability of an individual should not be considered as given, being something dynamic that changes according to both subjective and contextual factors. Moreover, the book hypothesizes that integrating dimensions and perspectives that have been so far overlooked by mainstream research will help deconstruct responsible behaviors adopting a flexible and holistic approach. Relevant policy implications are discussed, and empirical research on responsible behaviors is illustrated.

This book will be of great interest to students and scholars of consumer behavior, sustainable consumption, environmental psychology and environmental studies in general.

Pietro Lanzini is Assistant Professor at the Department of Management of Ca' Foscari University in Venice, Italy, where he gained his PhD in 2013. He obtained a MS in business economics and a post-lauream Master cum laude at Bocconi University in Milan, where he worked from 2003 to 2009 as junior researcher at IEFE and SPACE research centers. His international experiences include four months at the United Nations Headquarters in New York City (UNDESA, Division for Sustainable Development) and one year at the University of Aarhus in Denmark. His research interests focus on consumer behavior in the field of sustainability, and specifically on mobility and on spillover-related phenomena.

Routledge – SCORAI Studies in Sustainable Consumption

Comprising edited collections, co-authored volumes and single-author monographs, *Routledge-SCORAI Studies in Sustainable Consumption* aims to advance conceptual and empirical contributions to this new and important field of study. In particular, this series will explore key issues such as the emergence of new modes of household provisioning, the evolution toward post-consumerist systems of social organization, novel approaches to consumption governance and innovative business models for sustainable lifestyles.

The Sustainable Consumption Research and Action Initiative (SCORAI) is an international knowledge network of approximately 1000 scholars and policy practitioners working at the interface of material consumption, human well-being, and technological and cultural change. For more information about SCORAI and its activities please visit www.scorai.org.

Series Editors

Maurie J. Cohen, Professor of Sustainability Studies and Director of the Program in Science, Technology, and Society in the Department of Humanities at the New Jersey Institute of Technology, USA.

Halina Szejnwald Brown, Professor of Environmental Science and Policy at Clark University and a Fellow at the Tellus Institute, USA.

Philip J. Vergragt, Professor Emeritus of Technology Assessment at Delft University, Netherlands, and currently a Fellow at the Tellus Institute and a Research Fellow at Clark University, USA.

Titles in this series include:

Social Change and the Coming of Post-Consumer Society
Theoretical Advances and Policy Implications
Edited by Maurie J. Cohen, Halina Szejnwald Brown and Philip J. Vergragt

Responsible Citizens and Sustainable Consumer Behaviour
New Interpretative Frameworks
Pietro Lanzini

Social Innovation and Sustainable Consumption
Research and Action for Societal Transformation
Edited by Julia Backhaus, Audley Genus, Sylvia Lorek, Edina Vadovics, Julia Wittmayer

Responsible Citizens and Sustainable Consumer Behavior

New Interpretative Frameworks

Pietro Lanzini

Routledge
Taylor & Francis Group

LONDON AND NEW YORK

earthscan
from Routledge

First published 2018
by Routledge
2 Park Square, Milton Park, Abingdon, Oxon OX14 4RN

and by Routledge
711 Third Avenue, New York, NY 10017

Routledge is an imprint of the Taylor & Francis Group, an informa business

© 2018 Pietro Lanzini

British Library Cataloguing-in-Publication Data
A catalogue record for this book is available from the British Library

Library of Congress Cataloging-in-Publication Data
A catalog record for this book has been requested

ISBN: 978-1-138-30277-8 (hbk)
ISBN: 978-0-203-73170-3 (ebk)

Typeset in Times New Roman
by HWA Text and Data Management, London

To my parents

Contents

Illustrations

1 Introduction

New perspectives in consumer behavior

This book deals with the behavior of people in an age where environmental issues have gained center stage in the debate on the unsustainability of current lifestyles and economic development, advocating for the shift to a new paradigm. Environmental awareness is indeed experiencing an unprecedented boost: new interpretative frameworks on consumer behavior, new trends and analytical techniques emerging need to be systematized to provide a holistic, well-structured view of such a complex issue. Consequently, behavioral studies in the domain of sustainability are experiencing a steady evolution – rapid leaps follow one another, with the introduction of new variables and the development of innovative methods to increase the accuracy of existing models. To keep up-to-date in such a turbulent environment, the approach adopted is to consolidate the state of knowledge in order to benefit both from past advances and those that inevitably will take place in years to come. These advances will fine tune the predictive capacity of the proposed famework, rather than setting forth its obsolescence. Indeed, there is no clash between the scientific literature, which proceeds by micro-specialization, and the day-to-day practice, where the operative approach to the discipline requires some cornerstones on which to build a holistic vision. This book therefore represents a useful tool for scholars, practitioners as well as those lacking specific knowledge on the technicalities of the discipline.

Understanding behavior has always been a challenge, and many approaches have been proposed with differing degrees of interpretative potential (Jackson, 2005). In recent times, we observe, on the one hand, an increase in complexity due to the rise of new drivers behind behaviors; on the other hand, new tools are conceived and developed to interpret and predict human behavior, and specifically those behaviors that are relevant from the standpoint of sustainability. This assumes particular relevance in current times, as global challenges and issues leave the niche of academia to top the priority lists of policy-makers and businesses.

To add complexity to an intrinsically composite topic, when it comes to sustainability, consumer behavior attains a structure of values and beliefs challenging traditional patterns. In other words, the *rules of the game* are different.

This book has its roots in the acknowledgment of this evolving and complex scenario, where both traditional and new interpretative paradigms need to be integrated to provide a useful lens through which it is possible to gain deeper understanding of pro-environmental behaviors. The ramifications of this issue are multi-level, encompassing behaviors and their explanatory variables, but also the very categories that are adopted to address the problem.

Let's consider intention and behavior: although interrelated, the two constructs are different and as such they should be disentangled and analyzed. The following example helps describe this intricacy, showing how intention and behavior affect different profiles (in different ways) in their daily activities.

A commuter goes to work using a bicycle and public transportation, as she feels it is important to promote the image of a successful person who cares for the environment. Then, at home and away from social pressures, she does not recycle nor does she pay attention to energy-saving or other environment-friendly activities. In another neighborhood lives a woman who has an interest in environmental issues and strong beliefs about how individuals should limit activities with detrimental impacts on nature. However, she does not buy eco-labeled products as she cannot afford to pay the premium price, and takes her two daughters to school every morning driving a second-hand, highly polluting car.

Different drivers, different contexts, different *shades of green*. And, as a consequence, challenging questions to be answered: to what extent can we be effective with respect to these profiles in order to consolidate pro-environmental behaviors? Who is more reactive to which policies? Decision-makers have a wide set of strategies to orient behaviors, ranging from awareness to functionality, from praise to economic incentives, and so on. The effectiveness of such strategies can be (and usually is) asymmetric between individuals. Therefore, understanding behavioral drivers is a crucial step in order to make behaviors converge towards the envisaged objective.

Decision-makers are particularly aware of the complexity of the framework shaping individual responses to policies, and such a framework will be discussed in detail in the following chapters. The long list of drivers determining behaviors is somehow expressive of the high complexity of the policy–behavior relationship. A far from exhaustive list includes attitudes, values, perceived control, habits and past routines, availability of feasible alternatives, convenience, problem awareness, mutual interrelations between behaviors, perceived social pressure, socio-demographic profiles, monetary and non-monetary inducements, and so on.

Such complexity impacts the effectiveness of common policy issues, such as, for instance, interventions to reduce car dependence so as to curb traffic congestion and related air pollution. In such situations, which are subjects of great interest to behavioral scholars, the range of alternatives that can be considered to improve mobility patterns within the community is very broad, in terms of both their nature and their investment requirements. Overlooking the importance of behavioral determinants means neglecting an important effectiveness factor, which results in under-performing investment and thus a possible, or rather probable, waste of resources.

We are therefore confronted with several behavioral determinants on the one hand and implementation options on the other. As there is no *one-size-fits-all* intervention that is effective for all individuals, policy-makers typically adopt a panel of interventions that target specific segments of the relevant population. Some groups might pay more attention to the financial dimension of alternative transport modes, so that congestion charges or convenient public transport tickets might be an effective strategy. Other groups might be less sensitive to monetary incentives and rather privilege social acknowledgment or innovation *per se*.

The same line of reasoning can be adapted to companies interested in shedding light on how actual or prospective customers develop purchasing decisions, what is the role played by the sustainability of the offer and how can a firm exploit such knowledge in order to implement sound strategies from the standpoint of differentiation, pricing, communication, and so on. For instance, foodstore chain managers will decide on the visibility and role in the product range of eco-labeled, organic products with respect to traditional food without eco-labels. Moreover, they have to set the price range according to customers' willingness to pay for these two types of products. In this example, like in many others, decision-makers could benefit from a deeper knowledge of the drivers of responsible consumerism that help to take the most effective decisions.

Consumer behavior is interdisciplinary in nature, rating among the most-investigated issues within a broad range of fields including psychology, sociology, management and marketing. It emerged as a distinct field of study in the 1960s, and then developed through different stages.

Three traditional paradigms focus on the prevalence of a rational, behavioral or cognitive perspective and on the role of conscious and rational economic calculations, external environmental factors and information processing, respectively.

The *rational perspective* has its roots in the work of Adam Smith and Alfred Marshall, considering behaviors as the result of rational economic calculations where individuals act (e.g. purchase) in order to maximize their utility. Early studies mostly focused on purchasing behaviors, so that the main question to address was how consumers spent their available income evaluating the different alternatives that were available in the market.

The *behavioral perspective*, on the other hand, focuses on the role of external factors in our learning process. As the perspective shifts from the *inside* to the *outside* of consumers, there are relevant implications for business – marketing, advertising and, in general, all means of communicating and connecting with the consumer – which become key factors in orientating behaviors.

The *cognitive perspective* stresses the role of information processing as we pursue decision-making; individuals are problem solvers who are not blindly guided to purchase given products by specific advertising campaigns, as they actively seek, process and use available information to develop an educated choice.

These paradigms mainly focus on purchasing behaviors; indeed, the term itself *consumer* behavior clearly refers to activities connected with consumption. Since we are interested in the domain of sustainable behaviors, we need to broaden the scope of analysis so as to include activities that are not (directly) connected with purchases. In other words, we need to consider behavioral models that cross the boundaries of consumption and are able to explain how individuals develop behavioral choices in a wide range of domains.

The theories of reasoned action (Ajzen and Fishbein, 1980, Fishbein and Ajzen, 1975) and of planned behavior (Ajzen, 1991), which represent, in their original formulations, expectancy value models of decision-making rooted in theories of rational choice, did not develop in the specific field of environmental behavior, but proved to be useful in investigating the domain of sustainability. In response to growing findings of a weak correlation between attitude measures and later behaviors in attitude–behavior research, the theory of reasoned action suggests that attitudes (the personal desirability of a behavior) and subjective norms (representing social pressure) are the antecedents of behavioral intentions, which, in turn, mediate their impact and are the best predictors of behavior. Individuals are considered as rational beings processing available information to develop a conscious intention to act. However, in real life, many behaviors are not completely under volitional control, as both internal (skills, knowledge) and external (resources, facilitating conditions) factors play a role in shaping the likelihood of performing a given behavior. The theory of planned behavior is proposed as an extension of the theory of reasoned action which adds a third antecedent of behavioral intentions: the perceived behavioral control, representing the perceptions of how difficult or easy it is to perform a behavior.

Consumer behavior in the age of sustainability

Over the past 30 years, unprecedented attention has been devoted to the specifics of pro-environmental behavior and its drivers, given the relevance that sustainability has for policy-makers, businesses and society at large. Many factors contributed to this, ranging from anthropogenic disasters to sky-rocketing pollution, and from a growing awareness among consumers to demographic explosion. Catastrophes connected to the natural environment have occurred since the appearance of mankind (earthquakes, floods and fires), as did natural phenomena on large scale that heavily affected life on Earth (e.g. the ice ages). Moreover, mankind has always used technological advances to bring destruction in times of war and conflict, building and deploying powerful weapons. However, it is especially from the 1980s that catastrophic peacetime accidents directly connected with human activities (the Bhopal disaster in 1984 or Chernobyl in 1986) generated awareness of the limits that need to be put to economic activities (stringent safety regulations, prevention policies, pollution control).[1] It is no coincidence that this period witnessed some of the milestones for sustainability, such as the Vienna Convention on ozone layer (1985), the definition itself of sustainable development, known as the Brundtland Report (WCED, 1987), Agenda21 (1991) or the Earth Summit in Rio (1992).

As regards environmental degradation, post-industrialization pollution (from air and water pollution to acid rain, from the shrinking ozone layer to loss of biodiversity, and so on) reached unprecedented levels. While the list of the consequences of pollution and human activities is long, it here suffices to highlight that impacts are both local and global. A typical local manifestation is represented by emissions lowering air quality in large metropolitan areas affected by heavy traffic or large-scale industrial activity, with dangerous consequences for human health. On a global scale, pollution is causing the ozone layer to shrink and the climate itself to change: temperatures on the Earth vary (typically increase) at an accelerating pace, so that ice melts in Antarctica and Greenland, sea levels rise causing flooding, and extreme weather conditions become more and more frequent. Some figures can better illustrate the magnitude of these effects. Since 1900, carbon dioxide emissions have increased a shocking twenty-fold (and similar figures also apply to other polluting substances emitted into the atmosphere): the concentration of carbon dioxide in the atmosphere is now around 400 ppm (parts per million), and most simulations suggest that reaching the 450 ppm threshold would mean an increase of average temperature on the Earth of around 2°C. Deforestation is another crucial aspect of the impact of human activity on the environment, causing biodiversity loss, desertification, greenhouse effect and decrease in the carbon dioxide absorbed: since the 1990s, although the pace of deforestation seems to be slowing, we have lost between five to eight million (some say much more) hectares of forest each year. As regards the melting of the ice at the poles, every year 350 billion tons are lost, resulting in an 11 mm increase in sea levels since 1992. If the trend does not change, it is likely that salinity of the oceans will be altered, with catastrophic effects on weather patterns and sea organisms. Pollution and environmental degradation go hand-in-hand with the rapid demographic growth that has occurred in recent times, which, coupled with the affluence of lifestyles in modern societies, puts on a strain the stock of natural resources. The demographic issue is nothing new: Malthus (1766–1834) raised the question about the consequences of a population growing faster than resource availability in the late eighteenth century, at a time when global population was less than a billion. Population growth remained constant until 1900 (around 1.5 billion people), to explode during the twentieth century reaching 7.5 billion at present, with all projections agreeing on the trend to continue in the twenty-first century.

The complexity of the environmental degradation issue is reflected by the number of actors that are asked to play a role in shifting to a new, more sustainable paradigm: while business, policy-makers and citizens play a prominent role, the relevance of other players (from investors to non-government organizations (NGOs), from traditional media to the *web*, and so on) should not be underestimated. Firms need to change their overall approach to production processes and the way they do business, integrating environmental and social needs with the traditional economic dimension. While, until recently, most companies focused on the costs associated with cleaner production processes, adopting an end-of-pipe approach to comply with environmental regulations, they are now starting to see the business case for sustainability, and to consider the latter as a source of competitive advantage which must be managed proactively and pervasively. Policy-makers play an active role not only by setting standards and regulations to guide with a top-down approach the behaviors of citizens and firms. They are now adopting a cooperative approach, acting alongside other economic actors to provide them with the contextual conditions that facilitate the adoption of beneficial behaviors. Let's consider the case of urban congestion: traditional instruments such as congestion charges or so-called *ecological days* (where specific areas are closed to private cars) are still in use, yet being flanked and gradually substituted by other instruments. SUMPs (sustainable urban mobility plans) represent an example of public policy aimed at providing the contextual conditions for citizens to choose environment friendly transport modes because they *prefer* to do so (more convenient, enjoyable, etc) rather than because they *have to.*

Although many consider mitigation of environmental degradation the responsibility of the economic and public sectors, the role of individuals is crucial. People orientate businesses by means of daily purchases, rewarding (or not) those actors that demonstrate higher levels of environmental responsibility; individuals can pay more or less attention to resource savings in their household as well as in recycling activities, and so on. In most sectors, citizen involvement is a necessary prerequisite for any policy to be successful. Let's consider, for example, the case of mobility. Public authorities can adopt a top-down approach improving infrastructures or services: for instance, new bike lanes could be built and better public transportation systems could be implemented. However, any sustainable mobility policy needs an active role of citizens in order to be successful. No matter how frequent buses are, how many bike lanes are available: it is the single individual that each morning decides whether to drive her private car to work or university, or to take an alternative mode of transportation. In other words, it is necessary to improve the understanding of consumers, the key stakeholders in defining the success or the failure of both businesses and policy measures. Inconsistent results in prior research might be due to an oversimplification of a complex construct, so that it is necessary to investigate dimensions that have been so far neglected by mainstream research, stressing at once the need to adopt a holistic approach capable of considering the synergy effects of different drivers and the specificities of both the behavior at hand and the surrounding context.

This relevance is mirrored by the great array of contributions that emerged on the determinants of sustainable behaviors. However, although much has been written on the topic, it is difficult to delineate the mechanisms underpinning responsible behavior since different contributions have yielded inconsistent results. Proposed approaches (from simple socio-demographic-based segmentation to complex psychological models) seem to provide only a partial explanation of a complex phenomenon, with oversimplification of an utterly multi-faceted construct preventing researchers from reaching an integrated perspective. Individuals can act sustainably in certain contexts but not in others; they might hold strong environmental values yet have no opportunity to act accordingly, or on the other hand they might act sustainably for reasons that have nothing to do with feelings of social and environmental responsibility (because of perceived social pressure, or because it is more convenient in a specific context and situation). Many variables (both subjective and contextual) play a role in determining *when, if* and *how* we act sustainably. Since *we cannot manage what we do not know*, superficial analyses lead to ineffective policies targeting consumers and citizens. The deadlock that practitioners are confronted with represents the basis to answer a question that might arise when reading the first lines of a book on sustainable behaviors: *why now*. It is no easy task to provide a real contribution in a broadly investigated field where a plethora of books and articles have emerged over the last few decades. To represent a step forward in the ongoing discussion, the book needs to address some of the shortcomings of the existing literature and provide new perspectives crossing the boundaries of a mere collection of the current state of knowledge.

Research in a crowded field: how to contribute?

The novelty of this present contribution stems from differences in the perspectives of analysis with respect to the traditional approach to green consumers.

First of all, the problem with most of the existing literature is that it deals with a concept of green consumer which is not adequate in characterizing the multitude of possible orientations towards environmental issues. Individuals can act more or less sustainably and be more or less environment-friendly according to a set of variables, such as, for instance, the specific context (e.g. commuting to work or traveling to go shopping) or the role played at a particular moment (e.g. at work, rather than in private life). In other words, the analysis of the disposition towards sustainability of an individual should consider how such changes in attitude are affected by both internal (i.e. subjective) and external (i.e. contextual) factors. On this basis, instead of assuming the existence of a "green consumer" and studying only her distinctive features, this book analyzes the determinants of pro-environmental or pro-social behavior focusing also on those situations, conditions and mechanisms according to which the same individual acts more or less responsibly.

A second problem in most of the existing literature is that there is some confusion on the very basic construct of the behavior to be investigated. This book devotes a specific analysis to define pro-environmental, green and socially responsible behaviors as well as the subject of our analysis: green consumers, green citizens, ethical or pro-social citizens, ecological citizens, and so on. In the following chapter the choice of adopting the term *responsible citizen*, which covers a broader range of behaviors not only connected to consumption, is explained.

Third, a crucial aspect of this book is the proposition of a structured approach that builds on existing streams of research, gathering cues and conclusions from the multitude of contributions in the field and illustrating a perspective of analysis that integrates them. Usually research published in journal articles focuses on very specific aspects (i.e. few variables, a specific context, and so on); as such, it suffers from a destructured approach to the subject, only providing a partial answer on the determinants of responsible behaviors and focusing on single pieces of the puzzle:

none of the models ... adequately represents the multi-determination of environmental behavior on its own. Each model seems to over- and underestimate the importance of characteristic aspect

(Klöckner & Blöbaum, 2010: 574).

A premise of this book is that this step further consists in getting the whole picture, intended as the representation of the full set of interactions between the main variables involved in the process of responsible behavior (a comprehensive framework will be presented in Chapter 6).

Moreover, psychological theories are often considered to be in conflict with each other, rather than being different angles of the same construct. It is, however, important to consider the synergy of different theoretical frameworks, as decision mechanisms may vary according to the *type* of behavior (environmental, organizational, and so on), so that specific variables might assume greater relevance for some behaviors and situations but not for others.

Structure of the book

Building on existing theories and acknowledging the need to work on one single theoretical framework that is to be successfully applied to all behavioral situations, the book contributes to the debate by proposing a new interpretative perspective which specifically focuses on relevant dimensions (such as spillover mechanisms) that should be included in the analysis.

First, an overview on the state of knowledge in the field is provided. In Chapter 2, the reader is guided through an introductory discussion of complex and multi-faceted constructs such as responsible customers/ citizens and pro-environmental behaviors, a deep understanding of which represents a necessary prerequisite for the following chapters. This is crucial, as many contributions in the field use interchangeable labels that indicate different constructs, such as social vs pro-environmental consumer: since the two terms entail a focus on different dimensions of virtuous behaviors and ethical values, it is of primary importance to shed light on the differences and to avoid superficial identifications and overlaps. The term "responsible citizen" is then proposed as the core construct for the basis of the analysis. To provide a broad yet precise overview of how the topic of sustainable behaviors has been investigated so far, key existing theoretical frameworks are presented. Although the outline of the book will be limited to the main streams of research on the topic, it is worth stressing that models of consumer behavior in the field of sustainability are numerous, heterogeneous in nature and entailing different degrees of complexity (Jackson, 2005).

Early attempts of profiling a typical green consumer were based on segmentation-oriented approaches: research investigated which features (i.e. socio-demographic variables) identified individuals as acting green. The typical research method, therefore, consisted of surveys assessing pro-environmental behaviors and connecting them with a broad range of variables such as age, gender, income, and so on. Evidence emerging from such surveys might suggest that the elderly tend to recycle more than young people, that women tend to buy more organic food compared to men, and so on. Inconclusive results of these early attempts at investigating the determinants of responsible behaviors led to the formulation of models based on complex psychological theories such as the theory of planned behavior and also frameworks based on the concept of norms, such as the value–belief–norm theory (Stern et al., 1999), the norm-activation model (Schwartz, 1977; Schwartz & Howard, 1981), and many others, which will be described in detail in the following chapter. Furthermore, a different perspective of analysis stems from the assumption that often behaviors are performed as automatic responses to familiar and recognized situations, so that structured cognitive processes of evalutation of alternatives get deactivated, and habits emerge as crucial behavioral determinants (Verplanken, 2008, 2011; Verplanken & Aarts, 1999).

These approaches have been extremely useful in shedding light on the determinants and the psychological mechanisms underpinning our behaviors, albeit they encompass shortcomings and limitations that need to be addressed in order to improve our understanding of the topic. As such, they represent an essential starting point, the building blocks of further analyses and perspectives representing the core and the main contribution of the present work. Indeed, the book is conceived as a prosecution rather than a confutation of existing models, integrating and fine-tuning their consolidated body of knowledge.

The following sections of the book focus on three key elements in the investigation of the determinants of responsible behaviors, presenting in detail the theoretical foundations, the empirical investigations and the open questions that still surround them. Chapter 3 focuses on habits and the role they exert in affecting our behaviors. Why are routines and habits so important? Mainly, because once we *get used* to a specific behavior, this is carried out almost automatically, and we stop considering behavioral alternatives that might indeed benefit us. This is particularly the case of simple behaviors that are carried out repeatedly and in stable contexts. An example could be that of a man going to work by car: he drives five days a week, on the same route, at the same time. After a while, this behavior becomes so habitual that the individual will avoid even considering new alternatives, such as an improved public transport system that would make the journey more convenient, that might emerge. Psychological mechanisms triggering the development of habits are presented, as well as possible solutions to disrupt deeply rooted routines. The habit discontinuity hypothesis (Verplanken et al., 2008) is one of these: when habits are broken, there is a so-called window of opportunity opening up for behavioral change, which can be used strategically to promote desired shifts in behavior patterns. As a consequence, interventions are more effective when deployed within the context of major habit disruptions, such as those that occur in life-course changes: moving to a new town or changing job.

Chapter 4 focuses on the role of rewards (i.e. incentives), and bears relevant implications for advertising activities and public policies aimed at presenting a specific product/service or incentivizing the uptake of a specific behavior, respectively. It discusses the effect that these can have on intrinsic motivation and behavior, with specific reference to two types of external rewards: monetary inducements and praise. Since there is no general agreement on whether motivation to act can be triggered or hindered by external incentives, an overview on the ongoing debate is provided: the illustration of the main theories such as cognitive evaluation theory (Deci, 1975; Deci & Ryan, 1980) or self-determination theory (Deci & Ryan, 1985) and the empirical evidence available is followed by a discussion on the role that specific properties of rewards have in determining the impact on motivation and behavior. Recognizing the relevance that a thorough understanding of the relationship between different rewards and behaviors has for businesses and policy–makers wanting to implement strategies based on monetary inducements (discounts, promotions, etc.) or non-financial rewards (empowerment, praise and awareness-based communication), the chapter hence provides a useful guide with both a detailed overview on the topic and useful operational insights.

Chapter 5 illustrates the concept of pro-environmental spillover, which refers to the phenomenon according to which adopting a responsible behavior in one domain makes it more likely that other virtuous behaviors will be adopted even in distant and unrelated domains (Lanzini & Thøgersen, 2014; Truelove et al., 2014). The psychological mechanisms and related theories suggesting the existence of a positive (or, in some cases, negative) propagation of behaviors across domains are described and discussed in detail. Indeed, while the literature on spillover is vast, there is no general agreement yet on the existence itself of the phenomenon. Some scholars suggest (corroborated by empirical evidence) that different behaviors are not interrelated, so that what people do in one behavioral domain has no effect on other domains. For instance, if an individual starts purchasing more eco-labeled products, this will have no effect on other pro-environmental behaviors such as saving water and energy in their household, or adopting sustainable transport modes. Most of the evidence, however, suggests that behaviors are indeed correlated. But again, much research is still needed as there is no general agreement on the *direction* of the spillover effect. Some theories such as self-perception theory (Bem, 1972) or cognitive dissonance theory (Festinger, 1957) can be adapted to spillover literature to suggest that the adoption of a virtuous behavior makes more likely that other responsible behaviors will also be carried out (so that, in our example, if an individual buys green products it is likely that she will be more careful about recycling). On the other hand, perspectives such as moral licensing (Mazar & Zhong, 2010; Truelove et al., 2014) or contribution ethics (Guagnano et al., 1994; Kahneman et al., 1993) advocate the opposite effect, so that being responsible in a domain acts like a *waiver*, an excuse for being less attentive in other domains. Given the relevance of the topic and the uncertainties that still linger about it, a thorough description of available evidence and the strengths and weaknesses of different perspectives is presented.

Building on the existing body of knowledge, Chapter 6 represents the theoretical contribution of the book. To this end, it proposes a new interpretative framework suggesting new avenues of research and contributing to the current debate by a) focusing on dimensions that have been so far neglected by mainstream studies and b) analyzing the synergy effects of different drivers and the specifics of both the behavior at hand and the surrounding context. The framework describes in detail how the elements and the insights having their roots in different theoretical frameworks interact, shaping our behavioral patterns. Specific attention is devoted to elements playing a key role in such process, which are represented by the spillover effect and by the influence that habits and rewards have both directly on behaviors and indirectly on the propagation effect from one behavioral domain to the other.

Chapter 7 illustrates the details of research conducted on sustainable behaviors by means of a real-life intervention. The study covers all the key elements described in the book (from responsible behaviors/intentions to habits, from spillover to rewards, and so on), providing a privileged perspective to analyze how empirical investigations can be structured and implemented as to gather the informational background to be used by the new, proposed framework.

Note

1 It is however important to stress that *in nuce* environmental calls have been popular also before the 1980s, and numerous examples of safety regulations can be traced in earlier times

References

Ajzen, I. (1991). The theory of planned behavior. *Organizational Behavior and Human Decision processes*, 50(2), 179–211.

Ajzen, I., & Fishbein, M. (1980). *Understanding Attitudes and Predicting Social Behaviour*. Englewood Cliffs, NJ: Prentice-Hall.

Bem, D. J. (1972). Self-perception theory. *Advances in Experimental Social Psychology, 6,* 1–62.

Deci, E. L. (1975). *Intrinsic Motivation*. New York: Plenum.

Deci, E. L., & Ryan, R. M. (1980). The empirical exploration of intrinsic motivational processes. *Advances in Experimental Social Psychology*, 13, 39–80.

Deci, E. L., & Ryan, R. M. (1985). *Intrinsic Motivation and Self-Determination in Human Behavior*. New York: Plenum.

Festinger, L. (1957). *A Theory of Cognitive Dissonance*. Evanston, IL: Row Peterson.

Fishbein, M., & Ajzen, I. (1975). *Belief, Attitude, Intention and Behavior: An Introduction to Theory and Research*. Reading, MA: Addison-Wesley.

Guagnano, G. A., Dietz, T., & Stern, P. C. (1994). Willingness to pay for public goods: A test of the contribution model. *Psychological Science*, 5(6), 411–415.

Jackson, T. (2005). Motivating sustainable consumption. *Sustainable Development Research Network*, 29, 30.

Kahneman, D., Ritov, I., Jacowitz, K. E., & Grant, P. (1993). Stated willingness to pay for public goods: A psychological perspective. *Psychological Science*, 4(5), 310–315.

Klöckner, C. A., & Blöbaum, A. (2010). A comprehensive action determination model: Toward a broader understanding of ecological behaviour using the example of travel mode choice. *Journal of Environmental Psychology*, 30(4), 574–586.

Lanzini, P., & Thøgersen, J. (2014). Behavioural spillover in the environmental domain: an intervention study. *Journal of Environmental Psychology*, 40, 381–390.

Mazar, N., & Zhong, C. B. (2010). Do green products make us better people? *Psychological Science*, 21(4), 494–498.

Schwartz, S. H. (1977). Normative influences on altruism. *Advances in Experimental Social Psychology*, 10, 221–279.

Schwartz, S. H., & Howard, J. A. (1981). A normative decision-making model of altruism. In J. P. Rushton & R. M. Sorrentino (eds), *Altruism and Helping Behavior*. Hillsdale, NJ: Lawrence Erlbaum.

Stern, P. C., Dietz, T., Abel, T., Guagnano, G. A., & Kalof, L. (1999). A value-belief-norm theory of support for social movements: The case of environmentalism. *Human Ecology Review*, 6(2), 81–97.

Truelove, H. B., Carrico, A. R., Weber, E. U., Raimi, K. T., & Vandenbergh, M. P. (2014). Positive and negative spillover of pro-environmental behavior: An integrative review and theoretical framework. *Global Environmental Change*, 29, 127–138.

Verplanken, B. (2008). Habit and consumer behavior: Implications for interventions and behavior change. In A.Y. Lee & D. Soman (eds) *ACR North American Advances*, vol. 35. Duluth, MN: Association for Consumer Research.

Verplanken, B. (2011). Old habits and new routes to sustainable behaviour. In L. Whitmarsh, S. O'Neill, & I. Lorenzoni (eds) *Engaging the Public with Climate Change: Behaviour Change and Communication*. London: Routledge.

Verplanken, B., & Aarts, H. (1999). Habit, attitude, and planned behaviour: is habit an empty construct or an interesting case of goal-directed automaticity? *European Review of Social Psychology*, 10(1), 101–134.

Verplanken, B., Walker, I., Davis, A., & Jurasek, M. (2008). Context change and travel mode choice: Combining the habit discontinuity and self-activation hypotheses. *Journal of Environmental Psychology*, 28(2), 121–127.

WCED (World Commission on Environment and Development) (1987). *Our Common Future*. Oxford: Oxford University Press.

2 From green consumers to responsible citizens

Labels matter: the concept of *responsible citizens*

A preliminary definition of the object of analysis is crucial, as the literature on sustainable behaviors is full of contributions focusing on different types of activities (e.g. purchasing, recycling, sustainable mobility, activism, curtailment, and so on) and adopting different labels (green consumers, ethical consumers, sustainable citizens, etc.).

Early research focused mainly on consumption activities, so that the unit of analysis was typically the "consumer". Even in this specific domain, many labels have been used to indicate consumers guided in their purchasing behaviors by drivers other than traditional dimensions such as price, convenience or functional quality: *green* consumers, *socially conscious* consumers, *ethical* consumers, and so on. While such labels refer to closely intertwined constructs, they are not synonyms. In adopting a consumer approach, the first step is represented by a clear understanding of the subject of analysis; the main dichotomy to be clarified is between green and ethical consumers. Green consumerism first emerged in the wake of the green revolution of the 1970s and the attention of growing segments of consumers on the environmental dimension of products and services. In the words of Hendarwan (2002: 16), green consumerism involves "beliefs and values aimed at supporting a greater good that motivates consumers' purchases", while Elkington and Hailes (1989) state that green consumers avoid products or services endangering the health of consumers or others, causing environmental damage during production, use or disposal, consuming disproportionate amounts of energy or even causing unnecessary cruelty to animals. Ethical consumerism is born out of green consumerism, but is different from the latter as it covers a broader range of issues and a more complex decision-making process: it extends the definition of green consumerism adding a focus on the *people* perspective, encompassing wider ethical issues ranging from labor standards to fair trade, and so on. The traditional distinction between *green* and *ethical* consumer is hence based on the fact that the latter is wider in scope, adding to the environmental perspective a social perspective that often becomes predominant. This shift of focus from the environmental to the social dimension is in line with the evolution over the past three decades of the overarching issue of sustainability. The end of the century witnessed the concept of sustainable development first introduced by the Brundtland Report (WCED, 1987) becoming mainstream, with the Rio Conference in 1992 and the so-called Agenda 21. Sustainable development is considered to be development that allows current generations to achieve their goals, without compromising the possibility for future generations to fulfill theirs. It is probably not by chance that sustainable development became a relevant issue in the public debate in the 1980s. At that time, pollution and a series of peacetime accidents (from Bhopal to Chernobyl) triggered awareness in policy-makers and the public at large of the risks both for the environment and for human health and safety of current trends of production. Environmental degradation and tragedies connected to anthropogenic activities were nothing new; however the scale of the problem, the frequency at which emergencies occurred and the unprecedented media coverage made sustainability more salient than ever before.

Stemming from the dichotomy between ethical and green consumers and widening the scope of analysis to non-consumption activities, this book adopts the definition of *responsible citizen* to indicate an individual who is guided in her daily behaviors *both* by social and environmental drivers. The reader should be warned that since many of the examples and the behavior-specific discussions throughout the book refer to consumption activities, the term "consumer" will be occasionally adopted, whenever suitable to the specific case. Yet, it is important to clarify that consumer behavior represents a subset (though a relevant one) of broader behavioral patterns performed by individuals.

If we consider a typical example of behavior with relevant impacts on the environment such as purchasing, behaving responsibly would imply being guided not only by traditional dimensions such as quality of products or convenience (both financial and not), but also by an evaluation of the impacts that the product itself (and its production process) has on the environment and on society at large. This means being still interested, of course, in the price of the product and its traditional quality; yet, at the same time other variables are likely to be considered, such as whether the product is polluting through its whole life-cycle (production, consumption, disposal), whether it has been produced in compliance with adequate standards regarding social dimensions such as fair labor conditions, respect for local communities, and so on. In this respect, the adjective "green" might be misleading insofar it conveys the message of an attention to the environmental dimension alone, while the social dimension indeed also plays a crucial role in shaping behavioral patterns. The same holds for different domains. If we consider mobility, a responsible citizen will not be only interested in price, comfort and time when choosing a mode of travel: she will also consider the environmental impact of her choice, so that she might prefer using public transport to get to work, though this might entail increased travel length and less comfort compared to a private car. The specific situation might affect the salience of either the environmental or social perspective; yet, the two dimensions entail the same dignity and need to be analyzed synergically. Indeed, the two dimensions appear to get more and more interrelated, so that focusing on one aspect and dismissing the other would provide a partial, incomplete overview hindering a deep understanding of the mechanisms driving consumer behavior. This represents a possible explanation of the inconsistencies in previous studies. As an example, if we focus on organic food purchase (which represents a typical instance of sustainable consumer behavior), a critical aspect is represented by its entire supply chain. In this respect, not only it is important to make sure that food is harvested and processed in a healthy and environment-friendly fashion (minimizing the use of chemicals and additives, or the consumption of water for irrigation). We also want to make sure, for instance, that workers at all levels of the supply chain have been treated fairly (e.g. fair labor conditions, no underage work), and so on.

Early attempts of analyzing sustainable behaviors

There is a vast literature addressing sustainable behaviors and their related features. Through the course of time, different perspectives of analysis and different labels have been adopted in research; for instance, the focus of early investigation was the so-called green consumer, with analyses based on socio-demographic features of individuals such as age, gender, income or education. In other words, studies were aimed at *profiling* the typical green consumer, answering questions like "are males or females more interested in sustainability issues?", "who purchases more green products, young people or older people?", and so on. Empirical investigations were easy to carry out, as all the information needed was some sort of (often self-reported) behavioral measure, to be then analyzed with reference to the above-mentioned demographic variables. While this approach is still adopted by current studies, it was mainly in early research that the correlation between socio-demographic features and sustainable behaviors was adopted as the main perspective of analysis. The goal of such correlational studies was a segmentation of the market so as to identify the features of the typical responsible citizen (or consumer), or at least to single out features that are common in individuals that are more likely to adopt sustainable behaviors. However, the predictive capability of such approach proved to be inadequate.

Let's consider for instance the gender issue which has been broadly investigated by studies on the determinants of sustainable behaviors. Most of empirical research suggests that men have higher environmental awareness compared to women; the latter, however, show more favorable attitudes towards social and environmental dimensions and tend to behave more in a environment-friendly manner compared to their male counterparts. Can we then draw a conclusion from evidence emerging in literature? Apparently, men are aware of environmental and social issues, yet they fail to *walk the talk* and act consistently, while women adopt sustainable behaviors, albeit they have little awareness about sustainability-related issues. Who can be regarded as more responsible? The answer to such an elusive question has to be: it depends. Not only because different studies reach heterogeneous results, but also because emerging trends differ based on the fact that we either focus on awareness, intentions or actual behaviors. As a consequence, as pointed out by prominent scholars (Diamantopoulos et al., 2003) gender is not a useful criterion to investigate the determinants of sustainable behaviors.

Age has also been singled out as a variable of interest. For instance, it can be speculated that the elderly are, so to speak, *wiser* so that they better understand the relevance of virtuous behaviors. At the same time, however, some might argue that young people grew up in a period when environmental and social issues became mainstream in education, political discourse and on the news, so that they have been exposed to messages linked to sustainability and this might be reflected in greater awareness and, subsequently, consistent behaviors. Indeed, evidence in the literature is once again contradictory and inconsistent (Wiernik et al., 2013). Table 2.1 reports some of the studies on the relationship between socio-demographic variables and sustainable behaviors, performed in the 1980s and 1990s during the popularity peak of such perspectives of analysis.

Along with demographic variables, many studies focused on the socio-economic status of individuals as an effective strategy to segment population and gain insight on the social and environmental friendliness of people. Income is one of the variables that received most attention; once again, however, evidence is not conclusive, as studies found either positive or negative correlation, or even no relationship whatsoever between income and environmental attitudes and behaviors. On the one hand, there might be speculations suggesting that rich people have a *consumerist* lifestyle that encompasses a relevant footprint on the environment, so that they behave

Table 2.1 Socio-demographics and sustainable behaviors

Variable	Study	Sample size	Location
Age	Baldassare & Katz 1992	641	USA
	Grunert & Kristensen 1992	1,476	Denmark
	Pickett et al. 1993	460	USA
Gender	Schahn & Holzer 1990	167	Germany
	Stern et al. 1993	349	USA
	Van Liere & Dunlap 1981	806	USA
Education	Arcury et al. 1987	516	USA
	Berger 1997	43,000	Canada
	Witherspoon & Martin 1992	1,422	UK

less environment-friendly compared to low-income individuals. On the other hand, however, a counter-argument could be that the latter most of the time do not have the opportunity to undertake responsible activities involving extra costs. This could be the case, for instance, with green purchasing practices, since organic food or other eco-labeled products often entail the payment of a premium price that low-income individuals might not be able to afford.

As regards the effects of literacy/education, there is some consensus on the fact that there is a positive relationship with sustainable behaviors. The agreement however is not universal, as there is also research that finds either no or a negative literacy–behavior relationship.

Other variables have been adopted in the literature to investigate sustainable behaviors. Psychographic variables have been, for instance, the object of numerous empirical investigations, and seemingly outperform the predictive capability of socio-demographics. While an exhaustive overview of all different psychographic predictors of sustainable behaviors goes beyond the scope of this volume, it suffices here to note that these are large in number and heterogeneous in nature. For instance, altruism has been pinpointed as a relevant antecedent of such behaviors, though its beneficial effects are hindered on occasions where financial or behavioral costs are involved, such as purchasing organic food or green products. Furthermore, perceived consumer effectiveness emerges as yet another prominent behavioral antecedent; the more we feel we can make a difference, the more we are willing to take action. Environmental concern is a third construct that has been investigated, as there is a vast literature suggesting that environmentally concerned people have positive attitudes towards green purchasing, compared to individuals with no such concern.

Table 2.2 New Ecological Paradigm scale

Items
We are approaching the limit of the number of people the Earth can support.
Humans have the right to modify the natural environment to suit their needs.
When humans interfere with nature it often produces disastrous consequences.
Human ingenuity will insure that we do not make the Earth unliveable.
Humans are seriously abusing the environment.
The Earth has plenty of natural resources if we just learn how to develop them.
Plants and animals have as much right as humans to exist.
The balance of nature is strong enough to cope with the impacts of modern industrial nations.
Despite our special abilities, humans are still subject to the laws of nature.
The so-called "ecological crisis" facing humankind has been greatly exaggerated.
The Earth is like a spaceship with very limited room and resources.
Humans were meant to rule over the rest of nature.
Humans will eventually learn enough about how nature works to be able to control it.
If things continue on their present course, we will soon experience a major ecological catastrophe.

Scales have been developed to measure the construct. The New Ecological Paradigm (NEP) scale (Dunlap & Van Liere, 1978; Dunlap et al., 2000) consists of fifteen statements (or items) on which respondents are asked to express agreement adopting a Likert scale; it represents a widely adopted and reliable method for the assessment of the environmental world view of individuals and populations (see Table 2.2).

In order to understand the real motives underpinning sustainable behaviors, research should rely on more sophisticated models capable of grasping the inner determinants that actually explain how and to what extent individuals adopt virtuous behavioral patterns. This can be achieved by shifting the focus from simplistic (either socio-demographic or psychological) segmentation-based approaches to more complex decisional processes leading to behavioral intentions, and thus in turn to actual behaviors.

From reasoned action to planned behavior

Behavioral research in the field of sustainability can be broadly categorized into two main branches, rooted either in a rationalistic perspective or in the role of habits in triggering the suppression of an aware evaluation of alternatives, substituted by an automatic performance of behaviors. Whereas habits will be   subject of a specific chapter, the following paragraphs introduce the rationalistic perspective, which has long dominated research on sustainable behaviors.

Such a perspective assumes that behaviors are determined by deliberated cognitive processes, which are based on a rational evaluation of the information at hand and the available alternatives. A broad stream of research, reaching beyond the boundaries of sustainability, yet finding in this domain a fertile ground for theoretical speculations as well as empirical investigations, is represented by so-called attitude–behavior research. The theory of reasoned action (Fishbein & Ajzen, 1975; Ajzen & Fishbein, 1980) and the theory of planned behavior (Ajzen, 1991) with its further developments (Conner & Armitage, 1998) represent prominent theories that have been adopted in analyzing sustainable consumer behavior. Reasoned action has been broadly adopted in economic studies, and is close to traditional perspective of rational choice. The theory stems from the acknowledgement of a so-called attitude–behavior gap, which has a long track record of evidence in literature and posits that intentions represent the closest antecedent of actual behaviors. This, in practical terms, means that we do something because *we develop the intention* to do so. Intentions and actual behaviors are hence closely interrelated constructs, yet they are different and should be considered as such. When an individual intends to do something, it is likely that she will actually do it, yet this is not always the case. This happens because there might be some impeding factors (both contextual and subjective) that prevent the effective adoption of the behavior. For instance, I might intend to go to work by bike, yet at the very last minute it starts raining so that, although I intended to take my bike, I have to change my plans and drive the car.

Behavioral intentions are hence the main antecedents of actual behaviors. Intentions, in turn, have two main predictors: attitudes and subjective norms. Attitudes represent the positive or negative predisposition of individuals towards a specific behavior; they reflect beliefs towards an outcome (that is, beliefs about the likelihood that performing a behavior will lead to a given outcome) and the evaluation of such outcome (is it desirable, or is it something that should be avoided?). Subjective norms, on the other hand, indicate what we believe referent individuals or groups (henceforth, referents) expect us to do, hence reflecting social pressure. An example might clarify the two concepts. If we consider, say, the case of recycling, an individual might hold a positive attitude towards recycling glass, plastics and paper as she believes that this represents an effective way to support a worthy cause such as environmental protection through her daily activities. On the other hand, subjective norms reflect social pressure emerging if, for instance, neighbors and family members all carry out careful recycling activities, so that our individual might perceive that her referents are exerting a sort of social pressure, and expect a given behavior from her. It is worth pointing out that attitudes and social norms not always go hand in hand. For instance, an individual might not hold positive attitudes towards a sustainable behavior such as recycling: because she doesn't care about environmental issues, she doesn't perceive the specific activity as relevant from the standpoint of sustainability, and so on. Yet, she might still perceive social pressure because people in her social network think differently, and expect her to act accordingly. So, in this specific case, there is an absence of positive attitudes, yet the presence of subjective norms. This theory has been exposed to criticism for two main reasons. First, it appears to be an oversimplification, focusing only on two antecedents of behavioral intentions; in other words, intentions entail the intertwining effect of a wide set of variables that cannot be reduced to generic attitudes and social pressure. Second, the theory assumes that behaviors are under volitional control: individuals are considered as rational beings always capable of developing a conscious and elaborated intention to act based on the information at hand. Indeed, it is realistic to assume that there are both internal (e.g. skills) and contextual factors that impact the likelihood of performing given activities. Sometimes, we would like to do something (positive attitudes), and we know that people would praise us for doing that (subjective norms), and yet we still do not perform that specific activity. I might believe recycling activities are important and good for the environment and society at large and I might know that my referents carefully recycle and expect me to do the same, yet I do not act consistently with my attitudes and subjective norms (or at least not entirely). To overcome this limitation, the theory of planned behavior extended the theory of reasoned action by incorporating so-called perceived behavioral control as a third antecedent of behavioral intentions, representing the perceived difficulty related to the implementation of a given activity. With reference to the example on recycling, perceived behavioral control implies that an individual holding positive attitudes and experiencing social pressure towards the activity might fail to act accordingly because she believes recycling is a complex task that she does not know how to carry out correctly: she doesn't know where the recycling bins are, or she doesn't know how a plastic bottle with a paper tag should be collected. The theory of planned behavior has become a popular framework also in marketing studies, and is widely adopted to investigate behaviors in a wide range of domains, including responsible behaviors. The predictive capability of the model is good, yet the theory of planned behavior has also been criticized for the exclusive focus on three antecedents of intentions and behaviors; many authors indeed suggested the inclusion of further predictors (Conner & Armitage, 1998). Indeed, although planned-behavior frameworks do not represent a novelty in consumer behavior studies, they act like a living organism, as current research is still working on the original formulation, adding variables capable of fine-tuning the model and increasing its predictive capability. Some of such variables are particularly relevant in sustainability-sensitive domains. For instance, activities such as commuting or recycling are carried out repetitively in stable settings: I go to work every day at the same time, on the same route, and so on. The repetition of an activity makes it habitual, so that an automatic response at the subconscious level is triggered (Ouellette & Wood, 1998). Chapter 3 will provide a detailed description of habits; it suffices here to mention that they have been incorporated by many studies within the theory of planned behavior framework, and integrated as an extension of the original formulation. Furthermore, other variables are included in addition with the original constructs, such as anticipated affect (Ajzen & Sheikh, 2013), emotions (Fishbein & Ajzen, 2011), descriptive norms (Donald et al., 2014), and many more.

Values, norms and other psychological models

The theory of planned behavior probably represents the most widely adopted theoretical framework investigating behaviors that are the object of the present book. However, a wide range of heterogeneous models have been proposed to shed light on how individuals develop specific behavioral patterns. Without presumption of completeness, some models that are particularly fit for analyses in the sustainability domain can be summarized here. The norm-activation model (or theory) (Schwartz, 1977; Schwartz & Howard, 1981) was first developed in research on pro-social behaviors, but has been later extended as to analyze pro-environmental behaviors as well. According to the norm-activation model, personal norms represent the driving force of behavior. They consist of "feelings of moral obligation to perform or refrain from specific actions" (Schwartz & Howard, 1981: 191): individuals tend to act responsibly once they are aware of the consequences of their actions on the natural and/or social environment (that is, when their actions affect other people or the biosphere). The theory holds that there are situational variables that *activate* (norm-activation) personal norms, the most relevant of which are problem awareness and ascription of responsibility. Problem awareness refers to the extent to which an individual is aware of the negative consequences of not acting pro-socially, while ascription of responsibility reflects personal feelings of responsibility for such consequences. A wide body of empirical evidence supports the norm-activation model as many studies and data confirm its hypotheses

(Guagnano, 1995; Guagnano et al., 1994; Stern et al., 1985). It is curious to note that two different interpretations of the model have emerged. On the one hand, some scholars suggest that awareness of consequences is an antecedent of ascription of responsibility, which is in turn an antecedent of personal norms, with the latter being the closest predictor of behaviors. On the other hand, other scholars assume that awareness of consequences and ascription of responsibility *moderate* the influence of personal norms on behaviors (DeGroot & Steg, 2009).

Another popular model for the analysis of the determinants of sustainable behaviors is represented by value-belief-norm theory (Stern et al., 1999). The constructs are linked by a causal chain of five variables, as "each variable in the chain directly affects the next; each may also directly affect variables farther down the chain" (Stern et al., 1999: 86). These variables are represented by values, the new ecological paradigm (NEP), beliefs about the impacts of a conduct on the environment, ascription of responsibility, and personal norms. While the reader is by now familiar with the building blocks of the norm-activation model and the NEP, it is important to clarify the concept of values. These, in the framework of the norm-activation model, are rooted in the work of Schwartz (1992, 1994), with further modifications to fit the concept into pro-environmental research. They can be operationalized as concepts that "pertain to desirable end states or behaviors, transcend specific situations, guide selection or evaluation of behavior and events, and are ordered by relative importance" (Schwartz & Bilsky, 1990: 878). As such, they are more stable and abstract than attitudes, and have the capability to influence them; while attitudes are composed of beliefs about specific behaviors or objects, values are broader, overarching constructs. An interesting speculation sees the theory of planned behavior adopted mainly when sustainable behaviors are viewed as angled towards self-interest, whereas value-belief-norm and the norm-activation model are adopted when sustainable behaviors have pro-social motivations (Park & Ha, 2014).

All these models are rooted in a rationalistic perspective suggesting that behaviors are the outcome of an elaborated cognitive process. However, sometimes such an aware process gets deactivated, and people perform activities that become habitual almost automatically. The role of habits is crucial in research on sustainable behaviors (Aarts & Dijksterhuis, 2000; Verplanken & Aarts, 1999): indeed, next chapter will be devoted to a detailed overview of operationalization and measurement of habits, and theoretical frameworks based on the role of habits will be illustrated. It suffices to anticipate here that such models, ranging from the attitude-behavior-context model (Stern, 2000) to Triandis's theory of interpersonal behavior (1977, 1980) or to the comprehensive action determination model (Klöckner & Blöbaum, 2010), represent attempts of merging in a single behavioral model both a rationalistic perspective and the acknowledgement of the role exerted by habits.

The need for further perspectives of analysis

Some concluding remarks can be made at the end of this chapter. First and foremost, this proposed overview on theoretical frameworks analyzing behavior in the field of sustainability has no presumption of exhaustiveness. Indeed, some theories have not been mentioned in the text so as not to overwhelm readers with a plethora of different models and frameworks (Jackson, 2005). The selection of models illustrated responds to the need to find a balance between an adequate overview of all models considered relevant for the object of analysis and to avoid proposing an overly-detailed description of all different theories on behavior, that would exceed the scope of the present volume and create confusion for the reader.

The literature can be split into two broad categories. On the one hand, early attempts of analysis based on market segmentation according to socio-demographic or psychographic variables. On the other hand, sophisticated theoretical frameworks that illustrate the key determinants of sustainable behavior and their interactions, based either on a rational cognitive process or on an automatic response to cues (or, in some cases, on the integration of both perspectives). The contribution of existing theoretical frameworks cannot be underestimated, with current research that fine tunes the predictive capability of models with the inclusion of further variables that integrate and refine the original structure. However, research on responsible citizens often reached heterogeneous results. This might be partially due to different methodological approaches, comparison of heterogeneous samples, and so on. At the same time, I argue that inconsistencies between studies can also (at least partially) be ascribed to an oversimplification of an articulated and complex construct, so that the inclusion of further elements (and an analysis of their synergy effects) is recommended. To this end Chapter 6 provides an overview of variables and dimensions that have been so far overlooked by most studies on the topic and should be taken into consideration in future research. Moreover, a new interpretative framework will be proposed and illustrated as to support practitioners wishing to analyze the antecedents of sustainable behaviors.

References

Aarts, H., & Dijksterhuis, A. (2000). Habits as knowledge structures: automaticity in goal-directed behavior. *Journal of Personality and Social Psychology*, 78(1), 53–63.

Ajzen, I. (1991). The theory of planned behavior. *Organizational Behavior and Human Decision Processes*, 50(2), 179–211.

Ajzen, I., & Fishbein, M. (1980). *Understanding Attitudes and Predicting Social Behaviour*. Englewood Cliffs, NJ: Prentice-Hall.

Ajzen, I., & Sheikh, S. (2013). Action versus inaction: anticipated affect in the theory of planned behavior. *Journal of Applied Social Psychology*, 43(1), 155–162.

Arcury, T. A., Scollay, S. J., & Johnson, T. P. (1987). Sex differences in environmental concern and knowledge: The case of acid rain. *Sex Roles*, 16(9), 463–472.

Baldassare, M., & Katz, C. (1992). The personal threat of environmental problems as predictor of environmental practices. *Environment and Behavior*, 24(5), 602–616.

Berger, I. E. (1997). The demographics of recycling and the structure of environmental behavior. *Environment and Behavior*, 29(4), 515–531.

Conner, M., & Armitage, C. J. (1998). Extending the theory of planned behavior: A review and avenues for further research. *Journal of Applied Social Psychology*, 28(15), 1429–1464.

De Groot, J. I., & Steg, L. (2009). Morality and prosocial behavior: The role of awareness, responsibility, and norms in the norm activation model. *The Journal of Social Psychology*, 149(4), 425–449.

Diamantopoulos, A., Schlegelmilch, B. B., Sinkovics, R. R., & Bohlen, G. M. (2003). Can socio-demographics still play a role in profiling green consumers? A review of the evidence and an empirical investigation. *Journal of Business Research*, 56(6), 465–480.

Donald, I. J., Cooper, S. R., & Conchie, S. M. (2014). An extended theory of planned behaviour model of the psychological factors affecting commuters' transport mode use. *Journal of Environmental Psychology*, 40, 39–48.

Dunlap, R. E., & Van Liere, K. D. (1978). The "new environmental paradigm". *The Journal of Environmental Education*, 9(4), 10–19.

Dunlap, R. E., Van Liere, K. D., Mertig, A. G., & Jones, R. E. (2000). New trends in measuring environmental attitudes: measuring endorsement of the new ecological paradigm: a revised NEP scale. *Journal of Social Issues*, 56(3), 425–442.

Elkington, J., & Hailes, J. (1989). *The Green Consumer's Supermarket Shopping Guide: Shelf by Shelf Recommendations for Products Which Don't Cost the Earth*. London: Victor Gollancz.

Fishbein, M., & Ajzen, I. (1975). *Belief, Attitude, Intention and Behavior: An Introduction to Theory and Research*. Reading, MA: Addison-Wesley.

Fishbein, M., & Ajzen, I. (2011). *Predicting and Changing Behavior: The Reasoned Action Approach*. London: Taylor & Francis.

Grunert, S.C., & Kristensen, K. (1992) The green consumer: some Danish evidence. In: *Annual Conference of the European Marketing Academy, Marketing for Europe — Marketing for the Future*, vol. 1. Aarhus: Aarhus School of Business.

Guagnano, G. A. (1995). Locus of control, altruism and agentic disposition. *Population & Environment*, 17(1), 63–77.

Guagnano, G. A., Dietz, T., & Stern, P. C. (1994). Willingness to pay for public goods: A test of the contribution model. *Psychological Science*, 5(6), 411–415.

Hendarwan, E. (2002). Seeing green. *Global Cosmetic Industry*, 170(5), 16–18.

Jackson, T. (2005). Motivating sustainable consumption. *Sustainable Development Research Network*, 29, 30.

Klöckner, C. A., & Blöbaum, A. (2010). A comprehensive action determination model: Toward a broader understanding of ecological behaviour using the example of travel mode choice. *Journal of Environmental Psychology*, 30(4), 574–586.

Ouellette, J. A., & Wood, W. (1998). Habit and intention in everyday life: The multiple processes by which past behavior predicts future behavior. *Psychological Bulletin*, 124(1), 54.

Park, J., & Ha, S. (2014). Understanding consumer recycling behavior: Combining the theory of planned behavior and the norm activation model. *Family and Consumer Sciences Research Journal*, 42(3), 278–291.

Pickett, G. M., Kangun, N., & Grove, S. J. (1993). Is there a general conserving consumer? A public policy concern. *Journal of Public Policy & Marketing*, 12(2), 234–243.

Schahn, J., & Holzer, E. (1990). Studies of individual environmental concern: The role of knowledge, gender, and background variables. *Environment and Behavior*, 22(6), 767–786.

Schwartz, S. H. (1977). Normative influences on altruism. *Advances in Experimental Social Psychology*, 10, 221–279.

Schwartz, S. H. (1992). Universals in the content and structure of values: Theoretical advances and empirical tests in 20 countries. *Advances in Experimental Social Psychology*, 25, 1–65.

Schwartz, S. H. (1994). Are there universal aspects in the structure and contents of human values? *Journal of Social Issues*, 50(4), 19–45.

Schwartz, S. H., & Bilsky, W. (1990). Toward a theory of the universal content and structure of values: Extensions and cross-cultural replications. *Journal of Personality and Social Psychology*, 58(5), 878–891.

Schwartz, S. H., & Howard, J. A. (1981). A normative decision-making model of altruism. In J. P. Rushton & R. M. Sorrentino (eds), *Altruism and Helping Behavior*. Hillsdale, NJ: Lawrence Erlbaum.

Stern, P. C. (2000). New environmental theories: toward a coherent theory of environmentally significant behavior. *Journal of Social Issues*, 56(3), 407–424.

Stern, P. C., Dietz, T., & Black, J. S. (1985). Support for environmental protection: The role of moral norms. *Population and Environment*, 8(3–4), 204–222.

Stern, P. C., Dietz, T., & Kalof, L. (1993). Value orientations, gender, and environmental concern. *Environment and Behavior*, 25(5), 322–348.

Stern, P. C., Dietz, T., Abel, T., Guagnano, G. A., & Kalof, L. (1999). A value-belief-norm theory of support for social movements: The case of environmentalism. *Human Ecology Review*, 6(2), 81–97.

Triandis, H. C. (1977). *Interpersonal Behavior*. Pacific Grove, CA: Brooks/Cole Pub. Co.

Triandis, H. C. (1980). Values, attitudes, and interpersonal behavior. In H. Howe, & M. Page (eds), *Nebraska Symposium on Motivation 1979*, Lincoln, NE: University of Nebraska Press.

Van Liere, K. D., & Dunlap, R. E. (1981). Environmental concern: Does it make a difference how it's measured? *Environment and Behavior*, 13(6), 651–676.

Verplanken, B., & Aarts, H. (1999). Habit, attitude, and planned behaviour: is habit an empty construct or an interesting case of goal-directed automaticity? *European Review of Social Psychology*, 10(1), 101–134.

WCED (World Commission on Environment and Development) (1987). *Our Common Future*. Oxford: Oxford University Press.

Wiernik, B., Ones, D. & Dilchert, S. (2013). Age and environmental sustainability: a meta-analysis. *Journal of Managerial Psychology*, 28(7/8), 826–856.

Witherspoon, S., & Martin, J. (1992). *What Do We Mean by Green?* British Social Attitudes Report 9. Aldershot: Social and Community Planning Research.

3 The trap of behavioral patterns

The role of habits

Habits in consumer behavior research

The topic of habits can be introduced with a simple example of a common occurrence in which many readers are likely to recognize themselves. An individual drives on his daily commute from home to work, day after day, on the same route. Then, one day he is supposed to drive his wife to a new shop that is in the neighborhood of his workplace. He takes his car, and drives until he realizes that he missed the right turn – he was heading to his workplace, *out of habit*. He finds himself in a familiar situation (getting on his car, driving towards a specific area of the city he often commutes to), so that he does exactly what he is so used to, even if on the specific occasion he was supposed to go somewhere else. If we assume that some activities are performed automatically, with no rational evaluation of the alternative courses of action, the consequences are striking both from a theoretical standpoint (traditional frameworks focusing on rational cognitive processes overlook a relevant part of the story) and from a practical one (difficulties of reaching citizens and shaping their behaviors by means of marketing strategies).

I believe that habits represent an undervalued construct in behavioral research, with studies in the domain of sustainability making no exception to this; moreover, many activities which have impacts on the environment consist of habitual acts frequently performed in stable contexts, which represent conditions that facilitate the emergence of habits and thus their salience in orientating behaviors. Indeed, there is growing interest in the topic (both in terms of theoretical contributions and empirical investigations), with scholars in the field disputing over the role played by habits in shaping behavioral patterns. The debate is open, as there is still disagreement about the relevance of repeated behavior and its interplay with behavioral intentions as predictors of future behavior.

The implications are important for all those who want to influence behaviors with public policies or marketing campaigns. Let's consider, for instance, a municipality that is wishing to strengthen public transport in an effort to move to a sustainable mobility system. Awareness campaigns might see their effectiveness hindered, in cases where citizens do not rationally evaluate new alternatives nor seek or process new information available about new bus routes, new stations and the increased frequency of services. Similarly, a company selling organic food products might find it harder to reach potential customers with ads and commercials if most individuals go to the mall and automatically just purchase the type of food products they are used to buying, and that they have bought for a long time.

In contrast with the recent focus on how behaviors can be performed with little conscious deliberation, traditional models of consumer behavior assume that individuals do indeed follow a rational process of evaluation of alternatives, aimed at maximizing the expected value (utility) of a specific activity to reach envisaged objectives given the information at hand. Though we are far from the archetype of a *homo oeconomicus* and the rigid and unrealistic assumptions that characterize it, most of the widely adopted theories introduced in Chapter 2 are indeed rooted in a rationalistic perspective, where consumers (and individuals in general) decide their course of action based on a conscious process of evaluation of alternatives. The theory of reasoned action (Fishbein & Ajzen, 1975; Ajzen & Fishbein, 1980), for instance, assumes that individuals evaluate alternatives based on a conscious assessment of the desirability of given outcomes (attitudes) and an evaluation of how their referents will judge the person for performing such activity (subjective norms). It has been stressed that a first integration incorporated into the model is represented by the concept of perceived behavioral control that is based on the acknowledgement that often behaviors are not under volitional control. A further enhancement is represented by the introduction of habits. Sometimes behaviors are carried out without a conscious and rational evaluation of alternatives at hand; rather, they are performed almost automatically, without elaborated cognitive processes guiding our actions. We do certain things because we are used to do them; because it has become a habit.

Habits play a relevant role in shaping behavioral trajectories. Since this is especially the case of behavioral domains entailing relevant sustainability impacts, it is worth devoting a chapter of this volume to this specific topic. First, I will illustrate the concept of habits, providing an overview of the relevant building blocks and specifying why, albeit correlated, habits and past behavior represent different constructs. Second, since the recognition of the relevance of habits requires the capability of measuring them, a paragraph of the chapter will be devoted to an overview of some methodological approaches that have been proposed in the literature to assess both the strength of habits with reference to specific behaviors, and the generic predispositions of individuals toward developing habits. Third, I will illustrate why the development of habits is of interest not only for scholars and academia, but also (and, I would add, especially) for actors such as policy-makers and businesses that need citizens to adopt specific behaviors in order to fulfill their goals. Stemming from the relevance of habits to research on sustainable behaviors, I will discuss what can agents interested in changing behaviors do in order to disrupt deeply rooted behavioral patterns, or even replace them with new ones in line with the objectives of agents themselves.

Operationalization of habits

Habits represent a relevant element to be investigated in analyzing behaviors, as they have the potential of heavily affecting our choices. Although the term is commonly used in everyday language, a correct operationalization of the construct is no easy task. In common parlance, indeed, behaviors that are repeated over and over in a given setting are considered to be habits. If an individual checks his private email every evening before going to sleep, this is commonly considered to be his habit. Habits have arguably their roots in behaviors that are frequently repeated over time, with little evaluation of available alternatives. As such, a question that might arise is whether there is a specific threshold, or a minimum frequency of behaviors that signals the presence of a genuine habit. While some authors suggest that there are many variables that affect whether repeated behaviors develop into habits, so that it is a fruitless exercise to put a number on the frequency of the behaviors to determine the eligibility to habits, others propose specific conditions, such as behaviors repeated at least twice a month, or weekly, and so on. I personally believe that research should focus on the defining features of habits, rather than speculating on potential thresholds which, undoubtedly, should be flexible and vary across different behaviors.

Besides frequent repetition of the behavior, context stability also plays a role in facilitating the emergence of a habit. On the one hand, indeed, the more stable a context, the more likely habits are to develop and to have a direct impact on future behaviors. On the other hand, as contexts change, individuals are likely to consider different alternatives and seek further information so as to determine the proper course of action in the new situation at hand. Stable contexts play a relevant role, as individuals associate them with the mental representation of the behavior adopted in that specific context, so that the activity can be performed *automatically*, that is, with little or no conscious intent (Ouellette & Wood, 1998). The more satisfactory the outcome of the behavior, the more likely positive reinforcements (that is, rewarding consequences) are to develop and to strengthen habits over time.

It is now clear that the frequency of a behavior, the stability of the context and rewarding consequences represent preconditions for the development of habits. However, it is worth stressing that what defines a genuine habit is the way behavioral choices are made (Steg & Vlek, 2009). In the words of Aarts and Dijksterhuis (2000: 54) habits can be conceived as:

> a form of a goal-directed automatic behavior. Habits are represented as links between a goal and actions that are instrumental in attaining this goal. The strength of such link is dependent on frequent co-activation of the goal and the relevant action in the past. The more often the activation of a goal leads to the performance of the same action under the same circumstances, the stronger the habit.

The building blocks of automaticity and goal-orientation are present also in other well-established definitions of habits: these, in the words of Verplanken and Aarts (1999: 104), can be defined as "learned sequences of acts that have become automatic responses to specific cues, and are functional in obtaining certain goals or end-states".

Friedrichsmeier et al. (2013) propose distinguishing the habit concept between a *connectionist* (or *associationist*) approach, and a *script-based* approach. The former is rooted in the works of Wood and colleagues, and focuses on a stimulus–response connection – whenever an activity is performed frequently in stable contexts, an association forms between the representation of the context and the behavioral response. The script-based approach, on the other hand, is rooted in the works of Verplanken and Aarts:

> a schema or script represents knowledge of behavior sequences that are appropriate or expectable in certain situations, and can be triggered without first processing all aspects of a situation. Scripts or schemata then provide a blueprint for subsequent behavior
>
> (Friedrichsmeier et al., 2013: 2).

Scripts are particularly useful in low-involvement situations, as to minimize the effort sustained to collect and process information. The two concepts of habit, however, are not mutually exclusive and both processes could be effective at the same time.

An important caveat should be made in the distinction between past behavior and habits. This might appear a trivial issue at first sight, yet it bears relevant implications and deserves specific attention. Indeed, the need to disentangle the two constructs is made pressing by the fact that it is not uncommon to find studies that consider repeated past behavior as a substantial synonym of habit. Indeed, repeating a behavior over time does not suffice to state that a habit has developed. Better, repeated behavior represents a condition that is necessary, yet not sufficient, for the development of habits. As a matter of fact, an essential building block of habits is represented by *automaticity*. Triandis (1980), for instance, concedes that past behaviors and habits represent very similar concepts with significant overlapping and interrelations, yet he adds qualifiers such as *routinized* and *automatic*, defining the habit construct as situation-behavior sequences that are or have become automatic, so that they occur without self-instruction. Aarts and Dijksterhuis (2000) state that habits represent an automatic activation of a goal-directed behavior that restricts the set of viable alternatives considered by individuals in planning their activities. There have been also speculations on how specific features of the behavior at hand might impact on the concept of habits. Knussen et al. (2004) suggest that habits refer to simple daily behaviors (such as checking that all lights are off before leaving a house), whereas for complex behaviors the label "habitual behavioral patterns" is to be preferred.

How to measure habits

By now, most of the mist that surrounded the concept of habits and its correct operationalization should have vanished. Repetition, automaticity and stable contexts have been singled out as the three key features that define habits, which Verplanken (2011: 22) defines as "repeated behaviors that have become automatic responses in recurrent and stable contexts". A correct operationalization represents a propaedeutic step for sound management of the construct; subsequently, it becomes now crucial to develop effective tools to *measure* and assess the strength of a habit.

There is a long track record of evidence suggesting that habits develop as a consequence of a satisfactory repetition of behavior; consistently this led to the simplistic assumption that past behavioral frequency can be accepted as a proxy measure for habit strength. Indeed, early research considered habits and repeated past behavior almost as synonyms; whenever an activity was performed frequently, a habit was supposed to emerge. However, since most scholars (including this author) argue that habit is a psychological construct rather than past behavioral frequency (though the latter is a precondition for the development of the former), more elaborated assessment approaches have been developed.

The response–frequency measure of habit (Verplanken & Aarts, 1999) is framed as to present respondents with habit-related situations (e.g. travel destinations to work, shopping, favorite leisure activity, and so on), asking them to respond as quickly as possible to elicit the behavioral option that gets associated with the situation itself (for instance, taking public transportation, or driving a car). The response–frequency measure assumes that the more habitual the response, the more frequently it is chosen, so that the number of times a specific alternative is chosen can be considered as a measure of habit strength. The validity of the measure could be challenged by speculations that it might detect a general intention to perform the behavior, rather than a habit. A possible justification is represented by the fact that respondents are instructed to answer as quickly as possible, so that time pressure might deactivate a reasoned cognitive process, and make automatic elements triggering habits salient.

A more sophisticated index evaluating the strength of a habit is represented by the Self-Reported Habit Index (Verplanken & Orbell, 2003). Respondents are asked to express their agreement with a battery of twelve statements regarding a specific behavior, focusing on automaticity, repetition and identity. Table 3.1 reports the index with specific reference to the case of recycling.

It has been shown how there are objective conditions facilitating the development of a habit in an individual, such as the stability of the external context or the fact that a specific activity is carried out multiple times. It can be speculated, however, that different people react differently to such conditions. Are we all likely to develop a habit in the same way? The answer is no, as there are indeed people who are more inclined towards routines and habitual behaviors compared to others. In behavioral research focusing on habits, an important aspect is hence represented by the role that subjective features of individuals might play in shaping the development of the former, as the same context and frequency of the performance could lead to stronger or weaker habitual patterns in different people, due to their own personalities. Oreg (2003) developed a scale measuring whether individuals are attracted

Table 3.1 Self-Reported Habit Index

Recycling is something:
I do frequently
I do automatically
I do without having to consciously remember
That makes me feel weird if I do not do it
I do without thinking
That would require effort not to do
That belongs to my (daily, weekly, monthly) routine
I start doing before I realize I'm doing it
I would find hard not to do
I have no need to think about doing
That's typically me
I have been doing for a long time

to change, or tend to avoid it: the so-called resistance-to-change (RTC) scale. The work stems from the recognition of so-called sources of resistance to change that derive from personality traits of individuals. Such sources can be labeled as follows: (a) reluctance to lose control, (b) cognitive rigidity, (c) lack of psychological resilience, (d) intolerance to the adjustment period involved in change, (e) preference for low levels of stimulation and novelty, and (f) reluctance to give up old habits. Individuals are asked to state their agreement with a battery of statements dealing with the above-mentioned aspects. Although the original work of Oreg contemplated 44 items, most studies adopting the RTC scale focused on a subset of them. Table 3.2 represents an illustrative example of a revised (17 items) version of RTC scale that can be adopted in research on consumer behavior:

Table 3.2 Resistance to Change Scale

Routine seeking	I generally consider changes to be a negative thing
	I'll take a routine day over a day full of unexpected events any time
	I like to do the same old things rather than try new and different ones
	Whenever my life forms a stable routine, I look for ways to change it
	I'd rather be bored than surprised
Emotional reaction	If I were to be informed that there's going to be a significant change regarding the way things are done at work, I would probably feel stressed
	When things don't go according to plans, it stresses me out
	When I am informed of a change of plans, I tense up a bit
	If my boss changed the criteria for evaluating employees, it would probably make me feel uncomfortable even if I thought I'd do just as well without having to do any extra work
Short-term thinking	Changing plans seems like a real hassle to me
	When someone pressures me to change something, I tend to resist it even if I think the change may ultimately benefit me
	I sometimes find myself avoiding changes that I know will be good for me
	Once I've made plans, I'm not likely to change them
Cognitive rigidity	Once I've come to a conclusion, I'm not likely to change my mind
	I often change my mind
	My views are very consistent over time
	I don't change my mind easily

The RTC scale is hence designed to assess a general predisposition of individuals either towards change or towards developing deeply rooted habits. As such, it focuses on broad and overarching traits of personality rather than on specific activities or behaviors. Of course, there is a correlation between how individuals score on the RTC scale and on the Self-Reported Habit Index scale; it is reasonable to speculate that an individual that is generically averse to change will be more likely to develop habitual behavioral patterns in many domains. However, this might be (and typically is) not always the case. I could be inherently prone to change, yet be very habitual with respect to a specific behavior (or vice versa), for a broad set of contextual rather than experiential factors.

Some summary comments on this preliminary overview on habits can be now made. The reader is now familiar with the concept of habits, that a) represents a complex construct, b) which is connected to past behavior yet not limited to it, as other elements are necessary (automaticity, stable contexts, goal-orientation, etc.) and c) different definitions and scales have been proposed in literature to operationalize and assess habits and their strength. It has been argued that habits indeed represent a multidimensional concept, with behavioral patterns being based on associations between specific contexts and the activity, "that are elicited automatically upon encountering associated contexts" (Gardner et al., 2012). When habits arise conscious planning gets deactivated, norms and attitudes see their role in shaping behaviors weakened, and consideration of alternatives and the processing of information about them are no longer in place.

Integrating habits in a rationalistic perspective on consumer behavior

Habits often represent a relevant predictor of behaviors. Indeed, there are activities that, by their nature, are more likely to be subject to the rise of habits themselves; for instance, activities that are usually performed with daily frequency, in the framework of a stable context that remains constant over time. Many behaviors with relevant sustainability-related implications fall under this category. It is the case, for instance, of mobility, which represented the introductory example of the chapter; commuters go to work every day, Monday to Friday, on the same route, likely at the same time and in similar conditions (e.g. traffic conditions at a specific time of the day). Whereas little doubt should remain on the relevance of habits in determining (sustainable) behaviors, readers might at this point wonder what is the relative *weight* of habits in shaping sustainable behaviors, in comparison with other traditional antecedents such as attitudes and norms. On the one hand, it has been said that according to frameworks rooted in theories of rational choice, such expectancy-value models of attitudes and decision-making assume that habits have little relevance as predictors of behavior. On the other hand, it has been stressed how habits bear the potential of suppressing a conscious consideration of alternatives, triggering an automatic response to specific cues and stable contexts. These two assumptions, both corroborated by vast empirical and theoretical evidence in the literature, appear to be in contrast with each other. If we go back to the example of the municipality wishing to implement a new public transport system, the decision-makers might be interested in gaining insights on the determinants of modal choice in commuters. Since different works support heterogeneous hypotheses on the role, for instance, of habits in shaping behavioral trajectories, it is important to *put together* the results of multiple studies, to see which appear to be more robust and reliable. A statistical technique that can be used to this end is so-called meta-analysis: a meta-analysis synthesizes the outcomes of different scientific studies analyzing a specific phenomenon, like the role of specific variables in determining travel mode choice in our case. Lanzini and Khan (2017) conducted a meta-analysis on the psychological and behavioral determinants of travel mode choice. Habits, indeed, represent a crucial variable that plays a role of paramount importance in determining whether citizens opt for driving private cars rather than other, more sustainable transport modes (e.g. public transport):

> besides intentions, habits […] represent the main predictors, showing the highest correlations both with intentions and actual behaviors. Results corroborate speculations that especially in a domain characterized by stable context and settings such as commuting to work or to shopping […], there is a strong path dependency that heavily affects our mobility-related choices.
>
> (Lanzini & Khan, 2017: 16)

So, in the example of sustainable mobility, habits exert a role outperforming that of attitudes and norms (cornerstones of planned behavior frameworks) in determining how individuals act. The relevance of habits attenuates, in other words, the influence of attitudes and intentions on behavior; that is, "habits may function as boundary conditions for the validity of social cognitive models" (Verplanken, 2008: 125).

Consistent with acknowledging that habits and rational cognitive processes both represent determinants of behaviors, different attempts aimed at the integration of such approaches have been proposed. The theory of planned behavior, in its original formulation, has been criticized for assuming that behaviors result from reasoned considerations and a rational and conscious process. Indeed, behaviors might become habitual, so that a subconscious and automatic response gets triggered, and past behaviors interact with intentions in predicting behavior (Ouellette & Wood, 1998). Fishbein and Ajzen themselves acknowledge habits as a potential mediator of intentions; however, they relegate habits to a minor role. Ajzen (1991) actually recognizes that past behavior, once it develops into a genuine habit, has the potential to affect later behavior. However, he does not consider habit a causal factor in its own right: instead, he suggests that when we perform an activity a feedback is produced, which in turn affects attitudes and perceptions of social norms and behavioral control (the predictors of intentions and behavior, according to the original formulation of the theory of planned behavior).

The literature is rich in contributions and models based on an active role of habits in determining (sustainable) behaviors. Some of these, as previously discussed, have their roots in reasoned action and planned behavior frameworks (and intended as integrations and developments of the original formulations), others departing from the very assumptions underpinning such theories.

Thøgersen (1994) proposed an extension of the theory of planned behavior model where motivation (triggered by intentions, beliefs about outcomes, attitudes and norms) represents the antecedent of behaviors. However, motivation alone seems inadequate to explain individuals' behavior, as other dimensions ought to be considered, like the *ability* of individuals to carry out their intentions: "motivation leads to performance of the behavior only if the actor commands the required abilities to perform" (Thøgersen, 1994: 147). Ability (which has important similarities with the construct of perceived behavioral control) can be in turn operationalized into task knowledge and, indeed, habits, and it bears the potential to influence beliefs and evaluations that in turn inform attitudes.

Habits can also act as moderators of the intention–behavior relationship (Aarts et al., 1998); when an activity is repeated frequently over time, decisions are guided by habits rather than by rational evaluations of the alternatives at hand. Once established, habitual behaviors no longer require an elaborated process of reasoning or planning, since they are instead automatically evoked. Ronis and colleagues (1989) framed a theory of repeated behavior suggesting that the influence of habits on behaviors is independent of intentions, and repeated behaviors may be largely determined by habits rather than by attitudinal variables, although attitudes are central to the formation and modification of habits. Furthermore, Triandis (1977, 1980) proposed a model where intentions and habits interact in predicting behaviors – the so-called theory of interpersonal behavior. The theory has many similarities with Ajzen's theory of planned behavior, as they both include expectancy-value and normative beliefs constructs. The main difference lies in the fact that, while the theory of planned behavior states that behaviors are under conscious control, interpersonal behavior argues that consciousness decreases as the strength of habit in performing the behavior increases. Triandis's model can be hence conceived as a bridge between rational models and frameworks based on automatic responses to recognized situations. Intentions are described as a function of cognitive, affective and social factors, and the probability of performing an act is a function of intentions and habit, both multiplied by facilitating conditions. When an activity is performed frequently habit strength increases and, as a consequence, behavior is no longer guided by intentions. Indeed, habits can mediate the impact of reason-based concepts (intentions) on subsequent goal-directed behavior: the stronger the habit, the weaker the intention–behavior relationship. The underlying reason consists of the fact that, as a consequence of strong habits developing, the decision-making process underlying goal-directed behaviors either ceases to exist or significantly decreases; activities are performed automatically, with little consideration or elaborated cognitive process.

The attitude–behavior–context (ABC) model (Guagnano et al., 1995; Stern, 2000) is based on the dichotomy between attitudinal (i.e. internal) and contextual (i.e. external) factors, and assumes that stronger impacts of contextual factors will lead to a weaker attitude–behavior link. The four variables encompassed by ABC are attitudinal factors (e.g. values, norms etc.), contextual forces (e.g. incentives, external influences etc.), personal capabilities, and habits. According to the specificity of the case that is the subject of analysis, the relative relevance of each variable in guiding responsible behaviors can vary. For instance, travel mode choice is influenced more by policies and habits, while green purchasing is mainly influenced by factors such as knowledge or skills.

Also the comprehensive action determination model (CADM) (Klöckner & Blöbaum, 2010) advocates the integration of different approaches, since sustainable behavior can be influenced by intentional, habitual, and situational sources; according to CADM, moreover, intentional and habitual determinants can be in turn influenced by normative processes such as social norms.

Just as the theory of reasoned action and the theory of planned behavior are born out of environmental research, not all theoretical models and frameworks focusing on the role of habits as predictors of behavior are rooted in the literature focusing on the domain of sustainability. However, it should be stressed once again that habits can be particularly relevant for sustainable behaviors, since many activities with relevant environmental impacts are indeed habitual and well-practiced, like sorting garbage, or

Table 3.3 Habits and travel mode choice

Study	Outcome variable(s)	Sample size	Country
Chen and Chao 2011	Intention to use public transportation	442	Taiwan
De Bruijn et al. 2009	Behavior, use of bicycle	3,859	Holland
Donald et al. 2014	Behavior, car use vs public transportation	827	England
Eriksson et al. 2008	Behavior, car use	71	Sweden
Forward 2014	Intention, bicycle use	414	Sweden
Friedrichsmeier et al. 2013	Behavior, car use	1,048	Germany
Gardner 2009	Behavior, car use	107	UK
Klöckner and Matthies 2009	Behavior, car use	430	Germany
Lo et al. 2016	Behavior, choice of transport mode for commuting	386	Holland
Lois et al. 2015	Intention to commute by bicycle	595	Spain
Polk 2003	Intention to reduce car use	1,180	Sweden
Staats et al. 2004	Choice of means of transportation	150	Holland

commuting to work. Just to provide a snapshot of the long track record of empirical investigations in environmental research that focus on the role of habits, Table 3.3 presents a (non-exhaustive, and purely illustrative) list of papers that investigated the role of habits as predictors of behavior in the sustainability-related domain of travel mode choice.

How to disrupt deeply rooted behavioral patterns

The importance of habits in sustainable behavior, and the consequences for actors such as companies or public authorities attempting to shape the behavior of citizens, cannot be overestimated. The stronger the habit, the harder it is to "convince" citizens (by means of commercials, marketing activities, awareness campaigns, and so on) to change behavioral patterns, if these are not in line with the objectives envisaged by the agents. The suppression of consideration of alternatives and information processing is particularly severe. We can focus, for illustrative purposes, on the case of a municipality that is attempting to strengthen the public transport system. In order to do so, it increases the extensiveness and frequency of bus services and stops – more bus rides, better connections, shorter waiting times at stations. The success of such a policy depends not only on the actual efficiency of the new transportation system. If citizens hold deeply rooted commuting habits, as they are used to driving private cars, they will not consider the new alternative that is now available for them. Though the latter might be convenient, habit will prevent them from considering the changes introduced by the new policy, and prevent them processing such information that might convince them to shift to public transportation.

Both the relevance of habits and the implications for policy makers and businesses demand an answer to the following question: what can be done to change behavioral patterns that clash with corporate or policy goals, triggering at once the rise and solidification of new and virtuous habits? It is evident that the deeper habits are rooted in our everyday routines, the harder it is to change them. Some scholars have attempted to provide a solution to this dilemma, stemming from a basic assumption that activities that are performed frequently in stable contexts become automatic, and rational processes of evaluating alternatives get suppressed; changing habits demands solutions that disrupt stable contexts. There might be temporary circumstances that arise and limit habits, so that individuals are faced with the necessity to consider alternative courses of action. In the example of sustainable mobility, this could be the very case of commuters that choose, out of habit, a longer freeway route over a more efficient public transportation alternative. In the case of a temporary closure of the freeway for roadwork, many commuters might have to seek and process information about feasible alternatives; as a consequence, they might try the public transportation system and perhaps find out that this option is more efficient and comfortable compared to the old habit. In this case, even after the re-opening of the freeway, some commuters will find themselves *off-the-hook* of old habits, and decide to continue with the new, alternative course of action which might in turn develop into a new habit. The example of the closure of the freeway opens what has been called a *window of opportunity* for behavior change: individuals are set free from the trap of old habits, and are now free to rationally consider all feasible alternatives, to experience new options, and eventually to choose what fits their objectives best. The habit discontinuity hypothesis (Verplanken et al., 2008) indeed states that "behavior change interventions may thus be more effective when delivered in the context of major habit disruptions, such as those related to life course changes" (Verplanken & Roy, 2016: 128). In such windows of opportunity, individuals are more willing to search for further information about alternative courses of action, and are more open to change. When these discontinuities (e.g. relocation, change of job or family status, etc.) take place, individuals are somehow motivated to reconsider the way they do things, and are willing to look for information about the alternative opportunities. It is when these windows of opportunity open that agents interested in framing new behavioral patterns should deploy interventions, as they will be more effective compared to those carried out under default conditions. For instance, there is empirical evidence that providing citizens with free public transportation passes is more effective with respect to individuals who recently experienced a significant change in their lives, such as relocating or changing jobs (Thøgersen 2009). There is robust empirical evidence that supports habit discontinuity hypothesis. Some of these studies, for illustrative purposes, are listed in Table 3.4.[1]

Table 3.4 Habit discontinuity hypothesis

Study	Sample	Main findings
Bamberg 2006	241 citizens who recently relocated to Stuttgart	Significant reduction of car use and increase in public transportation after residential relocation and with financial and informational incentives
Brown et al. 2003	403 commuters in the University of Utah area	After a temporary parking shortage forcing commuters to use public transportation, many developed a new habit given high satisfaction for new advantages and benefits
Fujii et al. 2001	335 drivers in Osaka	The frequency of switching from car use to public transport during a temporary freeway closure is inversely related to the frequency of previous car commuting
Jones & Ogilvie 2012	26 commuters who recently relocated to Cambridge	Participants are open to changing their commuting behaviour following relocation
Thøgersen 2012	597 car-owners from Copenhagen	The effect of receiving free tickets for public transports was stronger in individuals that recently moved or changed workplace
Verplanken & Roy 2016	800 citizens from Peterborough, UK	After receiving an intervention to support the adoption of sustainable behaviors, bigger behavioral changes were detected in participants who recently moved house
Verplanken et al. 2008	433 Employees of an English university	Individuals who recently relocated were less likely to go to university with private cars
Walker et al. 2015	70 employees from an English NGO	Car use decreased after office relocation, slowly substituted by new habits (commuting by train) that gradually gain strength

Disruptions and context changes, at the same time, have relevant impacts also on people's values, attitudes and beliefs, making them more salient and people more attentive to them. It can be therefore inferred that habits affect behaviors with a double effect: on the one hand, they are antecedents of behaviors per se. On the other hand, they exert an influence on other behavioral antecedents (such as those of the planned behavior framework, or environmental values), so that they affect how these in turn shape behaviors.

With specific reference to the environmental field, some scholars have speculated on how to disrupt unsustainable habits and replace them with beneficial ones. The work of Dahlstrand and Biel (1997) is of particular interest. According to them sometimes habits are indeed functional, yet with detrimental impacts on the environment. This could be, for instance, the case of consumers that purchase polluting detergents as they cost less (and wash equally well) compared to their green counterparts. Purchasing commodities represents, like commuting, a typical example of behaviors that are performed in stable contexts, becoming habitual and being carried out automatically. To break the habit, authors suggest *unfreezing* the behavior, triggering the development of a new, desirable one and *freezing* it so as to become a new habit. The model proposed by the authors builds on seven consecutive steps which trace the process of turning an unwanted habit into a desirable one. Activation represents the first step; the attention of citizens is drawn to environment as a value, and such activation can be either generic (we need to preserve the environment) or specific (that soda bottles should be recycled with plastics). It can be inferred that the more specific the activation, the stronger the behavioral influence. Then, the second step consists of providing individuals with information about the negative impacts on the environment of current behaviors. A third step follows, where alternative courses of action are considered. The next steps refer to the fact that, in accordance with the chosen alternative, the new behavior must be respectively planned, tested and evaluated. The citizen at this point evaluates the new experience and, if satisfied with the new behavior, the final step of the behavioral change process towards a pro-environmental habit consists of the establishment of the new virtuous habit.

A couple of concluding remarks on habits can be outlined at the end of the chapter. Many activities that represent typical targets for a behavioral change in a sustainable direction are strongly habitual: it is the case, for instance, of modal choice, shopping, or even curtailment behaviors in our households such as energy and water-saving activities. The nature of habits (automaticity and lack of conscious intent, *tunnel vision* obscuring available alternatives, and so on) makes them particularly resistant to change, hindering the efforts of agents interested in encouraging citizens to adopt sustainable behaviors. Interventions aimed at shaping behaviors overcoming long-established patterns seem to be more effective when implemented concurrently with events that disrupt old habits, such as life-change events (relocation, change of workplace, marriage, etc.) or even temporary situations that force individuals to reconsider alternatives (the closure of a freeway, for instance). In these cases, windows of opportunity open and should be used strategically to promote behavioral change. In some cases, the substitution of old habits with new ones can be achieved by means of a step-wise approach based on the unfreezing of the former and the subsequent building of the latter, based on a new evaluation of alternatives at hand that are consistent with the envisaged goal and the value system of the individual.

Note

1 Some of the articles do not mention the Habit Discontinuity Hypothesis, yet focus on situations and research methodologies that are perfectly consistent with it.

References

Aarts, H., & Dijksterhuis, A. (2000). Habits as knowledge structures: automaticity in goal-directed behavior. *Journal of Personality and Social Psychology*, 78(1), 53–63.

Aarts, H., Verplanken, B., & Knippenberg, A. (1998). Predicting behavior from actions in the past: Repeated decision making or a matter of habit? *Journal of Applied Social Psychology*, 28(15), 1355–1374.

Ajzen, I. (1991). The theory of planned behavior. *Organizational Behavior and Human Decision Processes*, 50(2), 179–211.

Ajzen, I., & Fishbein, M. (1980). *Understanding Attitudes and Predicting Social Behaviour.* Englewood Cliffs, NJ: Prentice-Hall.

Bamberg, S. (2006). Is a residential relocation a good opportunity to change people's travel behavior? Results from a theory-driven intervention study. *Environment and Behavior*, 38(6), 820–840.

Brown, B. B., Werner, C. M., & Kim, N. (2003). Personal and contextual factors supporting the switch to transit use: Evaluating a natural transit intervention. *Analyses of Social Issues and Public Policy*, 3(1), 139–160.

Chen, C. F., & Chao, W. H. (2011). Habitual or reasoned? Using the theory of planned behavior, technology acceptance model, and habit to examine switching intentions toward public transit. *Transportation Research Part F: Traffic Psychology and Behaviour*, 14(2), 128–137.

Dahlstrand, U., & Biel, A. (1997). Pro-environmental habits: Propensity levels in behavioral change. *Journal of Applied Social Psychology*, 27(7), 588–601.

de Bruijn, G. J., Kremers, S. P., Singh, A., Van den Putte, B., & Van Mechelen, W. (2009). Adult active transportation: Adding habit strength to the theory of planned behavior. *American Journal of Preventive Medicine*, 36(3), 189–194.

Donald, I. J., Cooper, S. R., & Conchie, S. M. (2014). An extended theory of planned behaviour model of the psychological factors affecting commuters' transport mode use. *Journal of Environmental Psychology*, 40, 39–48.

Eriksson, L., Garvill, J., & Nordlund, A. M. (2008). Interrupting habitual car use: The importance of car habit strength and moral motivation for personal car use reduction. *Transportation Research Part F: Traffic Psychology and Behaviour*, 11(1), 10–23.

Fishbein, M., & Ajzen, I. (1975). *Belief, Attitude, Intention and Behavior: An Introduction to Theory and Research*. Reading, MA: Addison-Wesley.

Friedrichsmeier, T., Matthies, E., & Klöckner, C. A. (2013). Explaining stability in travel mode choice: An empirical comparison of two concepts of habit. *Transportation Research Part F: Traffic Psychology and Behaviour*, 16, 1–13.

Forward, S. E. (2014). Exploring people's willingness to bike using a combination of the theory of planned behavioural and the transtheoretical model. *Revue Européenne de Psychologie Appliquée/European Review of Applied Psychology*, 64(3), 151–159.

Fujii, S., Gärling, T., & Kitamura, R. (2001). Changes in drivers' perceptions and use of public transport during a freeway closure: Effects of temporary structural change on cooperation in a real-life social dilemma. *Environment and Behavior*, 33(6), 796–808.

Gardner, B. (2009). Modelling motivation and habit in stable travel mode contexts. *Transportation Research Part F: Traffic Psychology and Behaviour*, 12(1), 68–76.

Gardner, B., Abraham, C., Lally, P., & de Bruijn, G. J. (2012). Towards parsimony in habit measurement: Testing the convergent and predictive validity of an automaticity subscale of the Self-Report Habit Index. *International Journal of Behavioral Nutrition and Physical Activity, 9(1),* 102.

Guagnano, G. A., Stern, P. C., & Dietz, T. (1995). Influences on attitude-behavior relationships: A natural experiment with curbside recycling. *Environment and Behavior*, 27(5), 699–718.

Jones, C. H., & Ogilvie, D. (2012). Motivations for active commuting: a qualitative investigation of the period of home or work relocation. *International Journal of Behavioral Nutrition and Physical Activity*, 9(1), 109.

Klöckner, C. A., & Blöbaum, A. (2010). A comprehensive action determination model: Toward a broader understanding of ecological behaviour using the example of travel mode choice. *Journal of Environmental Psychology*, 30(4), 574–586.

Klöckner, C. A., & Matthies, E. (2009). Structural modeling of car use on the way to the university in different settings: Interplay of norms, habits, situational restraints, and perceived behavioral control. *Journal of Applied Social Psychology*, 39(8), 1807–1834.

Knussen, C., Yule, F., MacKenzie, J., & Wells, M. (2004). An analysis of intentions to recycle household waste: The roles of past behaviour, perceived habit, and perceived lack of facilities. *Journal of Environmental Psychology*, 24(2), 237–246.

Lanzini, P., & Khan, S. A. (2017). Shedding light on the psychological and behavioral determinants of travel mode choice: A meta-analysis. *Transportation Research Part F: Traffic Psychology and Behaviour*, 48, 13–27.

Lo, S. H., van Breukelen, G. J., Peters, G. J. Y., & Kok, G. (2016). Commuting travel mode choice among office workers: Comparing an Extended Theory of Planned Behavior model between regions and organizational sectors. *Travel Behaviour and Society*, 4, 1–10.

Lois, D., Moriano, J. A., & Rondinella, G. (2015). Cycle commuting intention: A model based on theory of planned behaviour and social identity. *Transportation Research Part F: Traffic Psychology and Behaviour*, 32, 101–113.

Oreg, S. (2003). Resistance to change: Developing an individual differences measure. *Journal of Applied Psychology*, 88(4), 680.

Ouellette, J. A., & Wood, W. (1998). Habit and intention in everyday life: The multiple processes by which past behavior predicts future behavior. *Psychological Bulletin*, 124(1), 54.

Polk, M. (2003). Are women potentially more accommodating than men to a sustainable transportation system in Sweden? *Transportation Research Part D: Transport and Environment*, 8(2), 75–95.

Ronis, D. L., Yates, J. F., & Kirscht, J. P. (1989). Attitudes, decisions, and habits as determinants of repeated behavior. In A. R. Pratkanis, S. J. Breckler & A. G. Greenwald (eds) *Attitude Structure and Function*. New York: Psychology Press.

Staats, H., Harland, P., & Wilke, H. A. (2004). Effecting durable change: A team approach to improve environmental behavior in the household. *Environment and Behavior*, 36(3), 341–367.

Steg, L., & Vlek, C. (2009). Encouraging pro-environmental behaviour: An integrative review and research agenda. *Journal of Environmental Psychology*, 29(3), 309–317.

Stern, P. C. (2000). New environmental theories: toward a coherent theory of environmentally significant behavior. *Journal of Social Issues*, 56(3), 407–424.

Thøgersen, J. (1994). A model of recycling behaviour, with evidence from Danish source separation programmes. *International Journal of Research in Marketing*, 11(2), 145–163.

Thøgersen, J. (2009). Seize the opportunity: The importance of timing for breaking commuters' car driving habits. In A. Klein & V. W. Thoresen (eds.) *Making a Difference: Putting Consumer Citizenship into Action*. Hedmark: Høgskolen i Hedmark.

Thøgersen, J. (2012). The importance of timing for breaking commuters' car driving habits. In *Collegium: Studies Across Disciplines in the Humanities and Social Sciences* (pp. 130–140). Helsinki: Helsinki Collegium for Advanced Studies.

Triandis, H. C. (1977). *Interpersonal Behavior*.Pacific Grove, CA: Brooks/Cole Pub. Co.

Triandis, H. C. (1980). Values, attitudes, and interpersonal behavior. In H. Howe, & M. Page (eds), *Nebraska Symposium on Motivation 1979*, Lincoln, NE: University of Nebraska Press.

Verplanken, B. (2008). Habit and consumer behavior: Implications for interventions and behavior change. In A. Y. Lee & D. Soman (eds) *ACR North American Advances*, vol. 35. Duluth, MN: Association for Consumer Research.

Verplanken, B. (2011). Old habits and new routes to sustainable behaviour. In L. Whitmarsh, S. O'Neill & I. Lorenzoni (eds) *Engaging the Public with Climate Change: Behaviour Change and Communication.* London: Routledge.

Verplanken, B., & Aarts, H. (1999). Habit, attitude, and planned behaviour: Is habit an empty construct or an interesting case of goal-directed automaticity? *European Review of Social Psychology*, 10(1), 101–134.

Verplanken, B., & Orbell, S. (2003). Reflections on past behavior: A self-report index of habit strength. *Journal of Applied Social Psychology*, 33(6), 1313–1330.

Verplanken, B., & Roy, D. (2016). Empowering interventions to promote sustainable lifestyles: Testing the habit discontinuity hypothesis in a field experiment. *Journal of Environmental Psychology*, 45, 127–134.

Verplanken, B., Walker, I., Davis, A., & Jurasek, M. (2008). Context change and travel mode choice: Combining the habit discontinuity and self-activation hypotheses. *Journal of Environmental Psychology*, 28(2), 121–127.

Walker, I., Thomas, G. O., & Verplanken, B. (2015). Old habits die hard: Travel habit formation and decay during an office relocation. *Environment and Behavior*, 47(10), 1089–1106.

4 Praise or money?

Rewards' effectiveness in shaping behaviors

An overview on incentives

The subject of the previous chapter – habits – represents a powerful construct capable of greatly affecting behaviors in a wide range of domains, including sustainability. One of the most problematic aspects of habits is that, since rational cognitive processes are deactivated, citizens are barely responsive to external information and stimuli, so that companies and policy-makers have a hard time in affecting patterns of behavior and eventually replacing long-established habits with new behaviors in line with corporate and public policy goals.

The present chapter, on the other hand, focuses on a dimension where external actors can be highly effective in shaping behaviors – it focuses on rewards,[1] and on the role that separate advantages, which could derive from performing an activity, might exert on motivation and behaviors. The implications are striking for communication and marketing; as a consequence, the present chapter will be of particular interest for those actors wanting to *reach* consumers and citizens with sound communications strategies to present their products or to sponsor specific behaviors.

Compared to habits, the perspective of analysis is entirely different. While these represent behavioral antecedents, rewards are not predictors *per se*. Instead, they are inducements being directly implemented by external actors, yet with a great potential of affecting citizens' behaviors both directly (incentivizing the behavior object of the inducement) and indirectly (affecting motivations that in turn inform behaviors).

Although rewards are widely adopted to incentivize a broad set of activities, they are particularly relevant for sustainable behaviors which often entail extra costs that citizens have to bear, whether financial or not. As far as the financial costs are concerned, a typical example is represented by the premium price that green products often entail; indeed, most of the time, organic food products and eco-labeled goods cost a little more than their traditional counterparts. On the other hand, behavioral costs need to be considered, as well. When opting for sustainable transport modes such as public transport, for instance, citizens face the inconvenience of having to reach the station or the bus stop, of having to adjust their schedule to bus and train timetables, and so on. As a consequence (although citizens might be still intrinsically motivated to behave in a sustainable manner) businesses and policy-makers often have to encourage people with extra inducements to offset these negative aspects.

Let's consider the case of a supermarket that is selling both traditional products (for traditional we mean products with no specific green label) and ecological products, such as organic food or products with an environmental certification. As the management is wishing to promote the purchase of green products within the store, two main strategies can be envisaged. On the one hand, citizens shopping at the store can be incentivized by means of monetary inducements. For instance, green products can be sold for a limited period of time with a 20 percent discount and so be more appealing to consumers, or they can be sold by adopting the typical "buy 2, get 3" scheme, or similar promotions. On the other hand, citizens can be encouraged to buy the green alternative by means of non-monetary incentives (praise rewards), such as awareness and praise-based messages in and out of store: for instance, messages focusing on the benefits (both for the customer and for the environment) of green products, like the healthiness of organic products or the contribution to the environmental cause made by choosing products with reduced emissions of chemicals and pollutants in rivers and environment at large.

Both strategies can have different degrees of success according to the personality of the consumer, the framing of the rewards, the type of products sold at the supermarket and many other subjective and contextual variables. However, the mechanisms underpinning the uptake of sustainable behaviors, when triggered by these two types of incentives, are different and have implications that are bound to affect future courses of action. The key aspect of rewards is their capability to affect motivation to adopt a specific behavior, and monetary and praise incentives indeed push different motivational buttons at an individual level.

Furthermore, rewards are typically offered to consumers for limited periods of time, for instance during a specific promotion. As such, their effect on behaviors (and on their determinants) are twofold. On the one hand, the immediate effect that lasts for the period of the promotion; on the other hand, a long-lasting effect that does not fade when economic inducements or praise have ended.

The effects of rewards on motivation

The crucial aspect of rewards is the impact that these can exert on motivation. According to self-determination theory (Deci & Ryan, 1985, 1991), intentions represent the closest antecedent of behaviors: people are indeed *motivated* as long as they intend to do something, to perform a specific activity, to choose a given behavior. In line with a rationalistic perspective, motivated behaviors are thus actions that are mediated by intentions. Motivation can be in turn labeled as intrinsic or extrinsic, according to the different reasons giving rise to the action:

> the most basic distinction is between *intrinsic motivation*, which refers to doing something because it is inherently interesting or enjoyable, and *extrinsic motivation*, which refers to doing something because it leads to a separable outcome.
>
> (Ryan & Deci, 2000: 55)

For instance, a student might be intrinsically motivated to study a specific topic because she finds it interesting, or she might have an extrinsic motivation of pleasing teachers and parents, although the study activity provokes no specific pleasure on its own.

In other words, extrinsic motivation arises whenever performing an activity gets triggered by its instrumental value rather than intrinsic enjoyment. An important aspect that bears relevant implications for research in the domain of sustainability is the role of rewards in affecting intrinsic motivation. The debate on the effects of rewards is still open (Deci et al., 1999, 2001): do rewards increase intrinsic motivation? Or do they, on the contrary, have a hindering effect? The controversy has now a long track record of opposing views on the topic, since the deeply rooted behaviorist dominance in motivation research, which would consider external rewards as strong behavioral motivators, has been challenged by cognitive explanations of motivation. The factors that determine variability in intrinsic motivation are illustrated by cognitive evaluation theory (Deci, 1975, Deci & Ryan, 1980); the underlying assumption is that we evaluate activities based on their ability to satisfy the fundamental need of being competent and in control. Self-determination theory and cognitive evaluation theory are similar, yet they differ, as the former incorporates the latter, being broader in scope. According to self-determination theory, needs for competence (or effectance), relatedness, and autonomy represent the three core psychological needs of citizens, since "people are inherently motivated to feel connected to others within a social milieu [relatedness], to function effectively in that milieu [effectance], and to feel a sense of personal initiative in doing so [autonomy]" (Deci & Ryan, 1994: 7). Cognitive evaluation theory can hence be considered a sub-theory of self-determination theory, with a specific focus on the factors that can exert a triggering or hindering effect on intrinsic motivation. The informational and the control aspects of rewards emerge as the key-factors in affecting intrinsic motivation. Information and control, indeed, can affect our self-determination and our perceptions of competency. Rewards may convey the message that an individual is competent; in this case, motivation would be clearly enhanced. However, rewards might also be perceived as controlling, so that motivation might be hindered by the uneasiness that derives from being controlled from the outside. It is the so-called concept of locus of causality, which refers to the degree to which we perceive our activities being either self-determined or driven from other agents: an external locus of causality arises whenever we perceive strong outside pressures. Going back to the example of supermarkets promoting green products, some rewards might be perceived as controlling, triggering an outward shift of the locus of causality, and a subsequent decrease in intrinsic motivation. For instance, individuals encouraged by either economic or praise rewards to purchase green products might perceive that they are not doing it for the environment, or for the inherent pleasure that supporting a good cause inspires. They might get the unpleasant feeling of being controlled from the outside, so that their motivation to act accordingly would be frustrated. The implications for marketing and communication campaigns are crucial: strategies need to be implemented and messages framed as to appear non-controlling to customers. The goal of the company has to remain in the background, whereas consumers have to feel empowered and in control, perceiving that they are acting with no external pressure. It is hence relevant to analyse whether the type of reward contingency is likely to be perceived as controlling or informational. Moreover, both aspects might be salient in a specific context, so that further elements should be considered so as to gain insights on the overall effect on motivation and consequently on behaviors (Deci et al., 2001). Although there is no universal rule that can be applied to all circumstances, most of the time praise rewards enhance perceived competence and subsequently motivation. Let's consider the case of a message that praises customers who are interested in a laundry powder: a typical message would focus on the fact that, by using an eco-labeled product complying with specific sustainability standards, the individual would help preserve the environment since the chosen product has, say, 50 percent less pollutants compared to traditional competing products, with evident beneficial effects on rivers, aquatic fauna and the environment at large. Such a message would provide an information background to consumers who feel more competent on the issue and, at the same time, feel good for being praised for their actions. This would not be the case for monetary rewards: a consumer who is incentivized to purchase an environment-friendly product only because it (temporarily) costs less would not perceive her competence heightened by any means, nor experience any pleasant feeling of being praised and approved. Indeed, tangible rewards such as monetary incentives are often (though not necessarily) perceived as controlling; in other words, they induce people to adopt behaviors that they would not adopt in the absence of the monetary reward itself, so intrinsic motivation is undermined. The general scheme (that, as previously suggested, should be handled with care as exceptions related to the contingent case are not rare) sees praise rewards as enhancing intrinsic motivation and financial rewards, on the other hand, as obtaining the opposite result. However, other variables need to be considered as they may affect the impact of rewards on motivation. For instance, rewards can be either expected or unexpected (Deci et al., 2001). The relevance of the distinction lies in the fact that rewards have motivational implications only if individuals are aware of rewards themselves (i.e. rewards are expected); if this is the case they may engage in an activity (also) to get the reward, with the well-known hindering impact on intrinsic motivation.

These illustrative examples pertain to the focus of this book and hence to the domain of sustainable behaviors. However, it should be noted that, like other theories on consumer behavior presented in Chapter 2, cognitive evaluation theory originally developed in the fields of educational research and motivation within organizations. Moreover, the theory does not focus on rewards only as variables affecting motivation, as many other external factors are examined, ranging from competition (Deci et al., 1981) to deadlines (Amabile et al., 1976), from evaluations (Smith, 1975) to externally imposed goals (Mossholder, 1980), and so on. Notwithstanding the original field of application, the insights of the theory can be adapted to different domains which are characterized by the interaction between rewards and intrinsic motivation, with environmental behaviors representing a typical example (Koestner et al., 2001; Pelletier, 2002; Thøgersen, 2003). Cognitive evaluation theory has also been criticized, with works (Cameron & Pierce, 1994; Cameron et al., 2001) denying the existence of an impact of extrinsic rewards on intrinsic motivation and suggesting the refutation of the theory. However, such contributions have been themselves criticized for flaws that make their results unreliable, and there is indeed a good track record of empirical investigations that support cognitive evaluation theory, in line with the results from Deci's seminal work on the issue (1971): one field and two laboratory experiments on the effects of rewards on intrinsic motivation confirmed that whereas monetary incentives hindered motivation and effort, verbal praise and positive feedback were able to strengthen them.

Consistent with cognitive evaluation theory, the over-justification effect (Lepper & Greene, 1975, Lepper et al., 1973) refers to the tendency of individuals to see their motivation weakened whenever they are provided with extrinsic reasons to perform an activity they would have done even without incentives. In the words of the authors:

> a person's intrinsic interest in an activity may be undermined by inducing him to engage in that activity as an explicit means to some extrinsic goal. If the external justification provided to induce a person to engage in an activity is unnecessarily high and psychologically "oversufficient," the person might come to infer that his actions were basically motivated by the external contingencies of the situation, rather than by any intrinsic interest in the activity itself.
>
> (Lepper et al., 1973: 130)

The basic assumption, once again, is that motivation (and the subsequent performance of an activity) is influenced by what we perceive to be the inner cause of our own behaviors. In case of external controls, we might ascribe behaviors to external agents, so that our motivation is weakened. Whenever we receive a monetary reward, we do not consider the behavior as self-initiated anymore, as we rather perceive it as triggered (also) from an external agent. In this case, too many justifications to take up a behavior emerge (i.e. overjustification); the role of intrinsic motivation gets discounted and motivation itself decreases.

Albeit that external rewards can potentially diminish intrinsic motivation to perform a task, the direct effect of rewards themselves should not be overlooked. A consumer might be less willing to purchase organic food products if she perceives she is being forced by external agents to do so, by means of monetary rewards. At the same time, however, the financial reward is indeed exerting a positive, direct influence on the behavior. The consumer in our example might see her intrinsic motivation diminished by the reward, yet she might still be induced by the discounted price to purchase the green product. So, basically, in the case of extrinsic rewards, there are two forces operating in opposite directions: the motivating power of the incentive and the decrease in intrinsic motivation (Frey, 1997). As a consequence, the overall effect depends on the relative strength of the two forces. The condition where extrinsic motivation triggered by external rewards is at odds with intrinsic motivation can be labeled as crowding-out (Frey & Jegen, 2001), whereas crowding-in pertains to situations when intrinsic and extrinsic motivation work in the same direction.

Implications for policy and business

This chapter illustrated how, according to a sound theoretical framework and a robust track record of empirical investigations, rewards that are perceived as controlling can hinder the intrinsic motivation to perform an activity. This is typically the case of monetary incentives and the hindering effect is particularly relevant for behaviors in the sustainability domain, given the salience of intrinsic motivation exceeding mere economic calculations. Most of the time, individuals tend to perform sustainable behaviors even if these also entail extra costs or practical inconvenience, because these factors are counterbalanced by a strong motivation to support social or environmental causes. Policy-makers and businesses wishing to promote the adoption of a sustainable behavior by means of rewards should be familiar with the main effects that these can trigger and that have been described in previous chapters. First of all, rewards weaken intrinsic motivation whenever they are perceived as controlling, while the opposite happens for rewards that make individuals feel competent. Most of the time, monetary rewards fall into the first category, while praise and information-based rewards fall into the second. Second, even if rewards hinder intrinsic motivation, the inducement could be strong enough to offset this impact, so that the overall effect determined by two opposing forces has to be considered. Third, it is important to consider the time dimension and whether rewards are implemented for a short period of time or, on the contrary, they last longer or even become permanent. Indeed, especially in the case of monetary rewards, it is likely that such inducements will have a direct effect outperforming the negative impact on motivation; however, once they end, monetary rewards might involve a backlash, with consumers not following the previously incentivized behavior because both the intrinsic motivation and the monetary inducement have disappeared. On the other hand, praise rewards might in some cases be less effective in the short term, yet display a better persistence over time.

The risk that actors, wishing to encourage sustainable behaviors by means of external rewards, will actually offset the benefits by weakening intrinsic motivation is particularly relevant, given the previously-mentioned salience of intrinsic motivation for behaviors with high environmental and social impacts. Particularly delicate is the possibility of the effects spilling over to other behavioral domains not affected by the reward in case individuals are not able to distinguish motivations according to different domains. Businesses and policy-makers should be therefore extremely careful in adopting pricing as a strategy to shape sustainable behaviors of consumers and citizens; the spillover effect to other behaviors might act as a multiplier of the detrimental impacts of the policy or marketing strategy, and could become more severe as the similarity of domains increases.

In conclusion, policy-makers and businesses typically resort to extrinsic rewards such as monetary inducements and praise messages as to incentivize people to adopt sustainable behaviors. Yet, although these often prove to be effective (at least in the short term), specific care should be made as motivation crowding effects and potential spillovers across behavioral domains should be considered so as to avoid counterproductive effects. This is especially the case of rewards that are perceived as controlling, such as monetary inducements, having citizens believe they are performing an activity for economic reasons rather than because of sustainability-related motivations.

Note

1 In this chapter other terms such as incentives or inducements will also be adopted interchangeably.

References

Amabile, T. M., DeJong, W., & Lepper, M. R. (1976). Effects of externally imposed deadlines on subsequent intrinsic motivation. *Journal of Personality and Social Psychology*, 34, 92–98.

Cameron J., Banko, K. M., & Pierce, W. D. (2001). Pervasive negative effects of rewards on intrinsic motivation: The myth continues. *The Behavior Analyst*, 24, 1–44.

Cameron, J., & Pierce, W. D. (1994). Reinforcement, reward, and intrinsic motivation: A meta- analysis. *Review of Educational Research*, 64, 363–423.

Deci, E. L. (1971). Effects of externally mediated rewards on intrinsic motivation. *Journal of Personality and Social Psychology*, 18(1), 105.

Deci, E. L. (1975). *Intrinsic Motivation.* New York: Plenum.

Deci, E. L., & Ryan, R. M. (1980). The empirical exploration of intrinsic motivational processes. In L. Berkowitz (ed.), *Advances in Experimental Social Psychology* vol. 13,. New York: Academic Press.

Deci, E. L., & Ryan, R. M. (1985). *Intrinsic Motivation and Self-Determination in Human Behavior.* New York: Plenum.

Deci, E. L., & Ryan, R. M. (1991). A motivational approach to self: Integration in personality. In R. Dienstbier (ed.), *Nebraska Symposium on Motivation: Vol. 38, Perspectives on Motivation.* Lincoln, NE: University of Nebraska Press.

Deci, E. L., & Ryan, R.M. (1994). Promoting self determined education. *Scandinavian Journal of Educational Research.* 38, 3–41.

Deci, E. L., Betley, G., Kahle, J., Abrams, L., & Porac, J. (1981). When trying to win: Competition and intrinsic motivation. *Personality and Social Psychology Bulletin*, 7, 79–83.

Deci, E. L., Koestner, R., & Ryan, R. M. (1999). A meta-analytic review of experiments examining the effects of extrinsic rewards on intrinsic motivation. *Psychological Bulletin*, 125, 627–668.

Deci, E. L., Koestner, R., & Ryan, R. M. (2001). Extrinsic rewards and intrinsic motivation in education: Reconsidered once again. *Review of Educational Research*, 71(1), 1–27.

Frey, B. S. (1997). *Not Just for the Money. An Economic Theory of Personal Motivation*. Cheltenham: Edward Elgar.

Frey, B. S., & Jegen, R. (2001). Motivation crowding theory. *Journal of Economic Surveys*, 15(5), 589–611.

Koestner, R., Houlfort, N., Paquet, S., & Knight, C. (2001). On the risks of recycling because of guilt: An examination of the consequences of introjection. *Journal of Applied Social Psychology*, 31, 2545–2560.

Lepper, M. R., & Greene, D. (1975). Turning play into work: Effects of adult surveillance and extrinsic reward on children's intrinsic motivation. *Journal of Personality and Social Psychology*, 31, 479–486.

Lepper, M. R., Greene, D., & Nisbett, R. E. (1973). Undermining children's intrinsic interest with extrinsic reward: A test of the "overjustification" hypothesis. *Journal of Personality and Social Psychology*, 28(1), 129–137.

Mossholder, K. W. (1980). Effects of externally mediated goal setting on intrinsic motivation: A laboratory experiment. *Journal of Applied Psychology*, 65, 202–210.

Pelletier, L. G. (2002). A motivational analysis of self-determination for pro-environmental behaviors. In E. L. Deci, & R. M. Ryan (eds), *Handbook on Self-Determination Research*. Rochester, NY: University of Rochester Press.

Ryan, R. M., & Deci, E. L. (2000). Intrinsic and extrinsic motivations: Classic definitions and new directions. *Contemporary Educational Psychology*, 25(1), 54–67.

Smith, W. E. (1975). The effect of anticipated vs. unanticipated social reward on subsequent intrinsic motivation. Unpublished doctoral dissertation, Cornell University, Ithaca, NY.

Thøgersen, J. (2003). Monetary incentives and recycling: Behavioural and psychological reactions to a performance-dependent garbage fee. *Journal of Consumer Policy* 26, 197–228.

5 How behaviors are interrelated

The spillover effect

Behavioral spillover, an intriguing concept for an open debate

As mentioned in the introduction to this book, behavioral spillover refers to the phenomenon and related psychological mechanisms by which the adoption of a responsible behavior in one domain affects the chances that other responsible behaviors are also adopted in other behavioral domains. In other words, acting in a responsible way increases (positive spillover) or decreases (negative spillover) a person's likelihood of performing other responsible behaviors.

This chapter digs into the details of the psychological mechanisms underpinning cross-fertilization between behavioral domains: the main theoretical frameworks supporting both positive and negative spillover hypotheses are illustrated, and an example of how spillover research can be conducted with a sound and robust methodology is proposed.

The actions of decision-makers are often aimed at shaping the behavioral patterns of a specific target. Businesses try to implement strategies to convince actual and potential customers to buy their products/services instead of those of competitors. Similarly, policy-makers tend to guide the behaviors of the community of interest towards patterns that are consistent with the envisaged objectives (e.g. increasing recycling to facilitate waste management, adopting sustainable transport modes to curb air pollution and road congestion, and so on). For these actors, the implications of behavioral spillover are strong; it is therefore relevant not only to analyze a single specific behavior in the domain of sustainability, but also to investigate how behaviors interact. For instance, if an individual purchases green products (e.g. eco-labeled products or organic food), one can speculate that, according to spillover theories, she will be subsequently more careful in recycling activities, in saving energy in the household, or in adopting more sustainable transport modes, with all the related consequences.

A first step for decision-makers is represented by acknowledging the fact that their actions (e.g. awareness campaigns or marketing strategies) bear the potential of influencing, and possibly modifying, broader behavioral patterns than those that are the specific target of the actions themselves. As will become evident in the course of this chapter, overlooking this aspect might have detrimental impacts on the effectiveness of their strategies, as decision-makers i) miss the opportunity to exploit the full potential of this propagation across behaviors, and ii) lack the knowledge and skills required to avoid the negative impacts that spillover mechanisms can trigger. Let's contemplate the case of a policy-maker considering implementing interventions within the framework of climate policies. Investment in such policies is warranted if promoting a specific responsible behavior raises the chances that other responsible behaviors are adopted too (i.e. positive spillover). If, on the other hand, the success on the behavior that is the object of the intervention is counterbalanced by a reduction in other responsible behaviors, the policy might be reconsidered and, perhaps, redesigned.

At present, awareness of the potential of spillover mechanisms is steadily increasing and most environmental campaigners are now considering how to include them in their strategies. This is the case, for instance, of the UK Department for Environment, Food and Rural Affairs, which sought "to promote a range of behaviors as entry points in helping different groups to make their lifestyles more sustainable" (Defra, 2008: 22). Actors other than public authorities are also active in environmental campaigning, such as NGOs and organizations such as the WWF, to name just one of the most world renowned. There is growing concern regarding the effectiveness of such campaigning, which often advocates for small changes in our daily behaviors, as every little helps: while not wishing to dismiss such efforts as insignificant, most observers suggest that if limited individual changes are pursued, the aggregate global effect will, likewise, be limited. This is where spillover can make a difference:

> Of particular importance for environmental campaigning is the related assertion that small pro-environmental behaviors can spillover into motivating more ambitious and environmentally significant behaviors. Thus, it is suggested, individuals can be ushered onto a "virtuous escalator", as one pro-environmental behavioral choice leads to another potentially more significant choice.
>
> (Thøgersen & Crompton, 2009)

The list is long, as heterogeneous actors are taking a stand. A report analyzing environmental campaigning recommends approaching individuals with "easy actions with obvious paybacks or pleasant effects that fit into existing routines, before building up to the more difficult ones" (Hounsham, 2006: 143). Moreover, Futerra (a consulting company focused on environmental communications) urges adopting foot-in-the-door techniques to trigger behavioral change:

> Get someone to do something small and then introduce another larger action once the small one is completed. The move upwards won't just happen on its own: communications are needed to link each rung of the ladder.
>
> (Futerra, 2006: 10)

Framing an effective strategy to support behavioral changes based on spillover mechanisms is no easy task. A policy intervention might, for instance, produce discordant effects on different behaviors, with both positive and negative spillover being triggered. As such, policy-makers should evaluate the net effect of an intervention after considering both negative and positive spillover, as jumping to conclusions without having a look at the broad picture (e.g. detecting one single instance of a negative spillover and, as a consequence of this, dismissing the intervention as ineffective) might be misleading and bring to superficial and inaccurate decisions. Let's consider the case of a municipality, an actor typically dealing with a set of critical issues to manage such as mobility and waste management. Policies in both behavioral domains require an active involvement of the population, which can ratify the success or failure of public policies with their everyday activities – being more or less attentive to recycling in the household, choosing public rather than private transport modes, and so on. The municipality has many options to address problems related to transport and waste management, with different effects (in terms of costs and/or time) and envisaged benefits to be assessed. The spillover hypothesis suggests that an effective strategy could be represented by focusing on the most cost-effective alternative, which is bound to act as a button that, once pushed, will induce a virtuous circle affecting also other behavioral domains. In our example this might be represented by an improvement of waste management, supporting recycling activities by means of awareness campaigns and tax benefits. This, as a consequence, might trigger psychological mechanisms convincing (at least to a certain point) citizens also to shift to more sustainable transport modes, *killing two birds with a stone*.

At first sight, the example can appear hyperbolic; yet the beneficial effects that spillover might produce require a thorough investigation of its existence and strength. Although spillover has been discussed in the literature and analyzed in empirical works for a long time, the debate is still open as research generated mixed and conflicting results. Many theories and theoretical frameworks (from unconnected literatures and different disciplines) have been proposed to suggest the existence either of positive or negative spillover effects.

Theoretical foundations for positive spillover

Focusing on arguments supporting positive spillover first, the main contributions can be ascribed to the concepts of identity, consistency and awareness.

As regards identity-based psychological theories, the one that has been widely adopted to investigate how behaviors are correlated is the so-called self-perception theory (Bem, 1972). According to self-perception theory, individuals use their own behaviors as cues to their dispositions: as we look at the behaviors of others to infer their attitudes, the same mechanism applies when we consider our own behaviors and attitudes. A spillover hypothesis can be derived from this theory (Scott, 1977): performing a responsible behavior might activate a broad disposition held by the individual (e.g. pro-environmental or pro-social values) that will likely influence future behavior even in other domains (Cornelissen et al., 2008). In other words, people taking up a responsible behavior develop, at a subconscious level, the self-image of a person who cares about the environment. As a consequence, this projection of the self will guide and shape future behaviors also in other, different domains – people infer attitudes from observing their own past behaviors and related contexts. The theory is not born out of environmental research, as it is broader in scope and can be used to analyze a vast range of behaviors. However, it appears to be particularly apt to describe spillover across pro-environmental domains, and many empirical investigations have been carried out which support its efficacy. Moreover, a self-perception explanation of spillover is consistent with the so-called foot-in-the-door paradigm (Freedman & Fraser, 1966), according to which individuals carrying out a small request first are more likely to accept carrying out a larger request later. The foot-in-the-door strategy has been applied and tested in several fields including responsible behaviors. However, it is worth noting that the self-perception explanation of the foot-in-the-door effect is still disputed as some scholars suggest that either there is no correlation between the two, or that the latter can account only partially for the variance of the investigations, as there is no direct evidence of a shift in individuals' self-concepts following foot-in-the-door manipulations.

Self-perception can be linked to identity effects, and specifically to what can be labeled as social identity. Specifically, social identity reflects the part of the self-concept of an individual that is based on the belonging to a specific social group. If we strongly identify ourselves with such a group, we develop a sort of obligation to act. We tend to act responsibly across behavioral domains because, once pro-environmental identity becomes salient, this identification of the self as a responsible individual from the standpoint of sustainability has people act accordingly, so as to avoid stigma and exclusion from the reference group. Identity thus mediates positive spillover effects, as:

> cueing people about the positive environmental outcomes of their behavior leads them to see themselves as the type of person who is concerned about environmental issues, essentially establishing an environmental identity and corresponding rules of conduct.
>
> (Truelove et al., 2014: 131)

Identity effects can be hence analyzed from two perspectives: a subjective search for consistency, driven by a depiction of the self as an individual holding strong pro-environmental and pro-social beliefs, and an externally driven quest for behavioral patterns matching those of the social groups we want to be part of. The latter dimension can be interpreted as the counterpart of what subjective norms are for planned behavior; a reflection of the perceived social pressure to adopt behaviors that are in line with what we are expected to do in given situations by our referents.

The search for consistency and the natural tendency of an individual to be consistent (and also to look consistent to his referents) represents a possible explanation for positive spillover on its own, and different consistency theories (Abelson, 1983) have been proposed as sound frameworks to explain the phenomenon. Cognitive dissonance theory (Festinger, 1957) has been widely adopted, having indeed its roots in the feelings of discomfort that arise when people behave inconsistently across behaviors. An example relevant to the domain of pro-environmental behaviors could be represented by how we would feel uncomfortable if, after adopting a responsible behavior such as purchasing organic food, we later do not act consistently in other domains, not sorting garbage carefully or avoiding sustainable travel modes.

Consistency drivers do not only refer to the subjective discomfort that inconsistent behaviors produce; on the other hand, social (i.e. external) motivations are extremely important, as well. Individuals who do not adopt consistent behaviors can be viewed as hypocritical and judged negatively, so that in order to project a positive image of a coherent and moral person, people are motivated to act consistently across domains, triggering a mechanism that produces a spillover phenomenon. A consistency-based explanation of spillover hence builds once again on the integration of an inner (avoid discomfort) and an outer (social image) driver. Each of the two, according to the specifics of the context, the behaviors and the individual can play a prominent role. For instance, the more the responsible behavior is carried out in public, the more salient the social driver is likely to be. The worst inconsistencies are those involving high priority values and self-concept; moral standards can hence influence how inconsistencies are perceived as disturbing by individuals. Moreover, it should be pointed out that behavioral shifts should be easy, else individuals might prefer other routes to avoid discomfort; for instance they might choose the unsustainable behavior in both domains as to get rid of inconsistencies.

Learning theories focus on the role played by awareness, knowledge and skills in triggering a learning-by-doing process. When individuals take up a responsible behavior, they collect information, they acquire skills and develop awareness on sustainability issues that imply an increased capability and willingness to adopt further pro-environmental behaviors. An individual who goes shopping, and who is convinced by health-related motives to ask for food products that do not contain traces of fertilizers or other potentially harmful chemical substances, represents a typical example. In doing so, he might become familiar with the previously unknown concept of certification (in this specific case, organic farming or biological product label). Curiosity about the topic would have our agent look for information on certification schemes, even for different product categories, so that it is more likely that he will consider eco-labels even when purchasing other non-food goods for which schemes of environmental or social certification are available (e.g. kitchen paper produced with paper deriving from sustainably-managed forests as certified by the Forest Stewardship Council) (see Box 5.1).

Learning theories are supported by vast amounts of empirical evidence predicting that engaging in a responsible behavior is likely to facilitate taking up other consistent behaviors given improved skills and self-confidence in sustainability-related domains, and the increased awareness of the issues. Some scholars, on the other hand, are more cautious on the potential of learning mechanisms to shape responsible behavioral patterns and even more so to initiate a virtuous circle encompassing spillover. The role of awareness should not be over-emphasized, they argue, as the track record of awareness campaigns in the environmental field is notoriously poor.

Goal theory (Dhar & Simonson, 1999) stems from the assumption that there are broad goals to achieve which different activities can play a role. Examples of such goals range from being healthy to integrating in our social environment, from enjoying pleasant activities to preserving the environment, and so on. If we focus on the overarching goal of

***Box 5.1* Product certification**

Product certification is a form of communication along the supply chain allowing buyers and all interested parties to recognize whether a product complies with specific environmental criteria. The tool has its roots in decades of so-called *greenwashing* phenomenon, with companies framing marketing campaigns based on deceptive business claims of eco-friendliness. Greenwashing led to a generalized distrust among consumers, who faced difficulties in discerning which products were actually green from those which only claimed so. An effective solution has been found in certification labels, awarded by (typically public) third-party bodies that, given their independence, are deemed to be more credible and reliable. To date, many initiatives and schemes both at national and international level have been developed. The number of different frameworks has been blamed as a possible hindrance for broader success of eco-labels, given the confusion they create in customers. Focusing on the European Union, there are different certification schemes that are either country-based (e.g. Blau Angel in Germany or NF Environment in France) or region-based (e.g. the Nordic Swan in Scandinavia). At the community level, the EU Ecolabel (established in 1992 by council regulation EEC 880/92 and now governed by regulation EC 66/2010) is a voluntary instrument based on a system of selective criteria, defined on a scientific basis, taking into account the environmental impacts of the entire life-cycle of products. The criteria have been established after a process involving a wide set of stakeholders including NGOs and consumer associations, and they address not only environmental aspects but also consumers' health and safety.

sustainability, there are many behaviors in our everyday life that can be adopted so as to contribute to the fulfillment of such a goal. We can contribute to the cause of sustainability by purchasing green products, recycling our garbage carefully, saving resources in the household with curtailment activities, adopting sustainable transport modes, contributing to a social or environmental cause either with an economic donation or with active volunteering, and so on. Clearly, it is very difficult (if not impossible) to adopt responsible behaviors in regard to all domains with relevant sustainability impacts, as an allocation of resources, which can be financial but also connected to time or effort required, is necessary. As a consequence, we tend to achieve the goal focusing on those activities that entail the least effort first. However, the implications for spillover mechanisms are relevant, as one can speculate that when an individual carries out a pro-environmental activity, the broad goal of sustainability gets primed, activating a propagation across behavioral domains by guiding other behaviors.

Theoretical foundations for negative spillover

Spillover can also be negative, if an intervention that is successful in increasing one responsible behavior produces a decrease in a different, sustainability-related behavior. Psychological mechanisms leading to negative spillover have been known for a long time: the economist William Stanley Jevons observed in his 1865 book *The Coal Question* that coal consumption in England increased after Watt introduced the (coal-powered) steam engine, which was more efficient than the Newcomen engine. Coal consumption increased as a consequence of an innovation that reduced the amount necessary for any given work (Box 5.2).

Box 5.2 **Jevon's paradox**

In environmental economics, the Jevon's paradox reflects the phenomenon occurring when, as a consequence of an improved efficiency in the use of a given resource, the demand of the latter increases because of a rise in its rate of consumption.

The paradox owes its name to William Stanley Jevons, an English economist who in his 1865 book *The Coal Question* observed that technological improvements increasing the efficiency of coal use caused the consumption of coal to increase in many industries, rather than decline. Specifically, he noted that coal consumption soared after the introduction of Watt's steam engine, which replaced the old and less efficient Newcomen's steam engine.

The implications are crucial. Contrary to common sense and to the mainstream opinion of policy-makers and environmentalists, technological progress is not likely to reduce the consumption of resources: if efficiency increases so that the amount of a resource needed for a given use decreases, companies are somehow spurred on to consume more, given the lower cost of resource use. The debate on the size of such rebound effects is still open. It has also been proposed to implement conservation policies and government interventions aimed at reducing demand, such as environmental taxes or so-called cap and trade mechanisms.

This so-called rebound effect has been object of empirical investigations in the pro-environmental domain. For instance, efficiency improvements in the household, such as the weatherizing of apartments, lead to increased temperature setting of the thermostat, and a subsequent decrease in energy savings. That is, a responsible behavior (that can be supported by policy measures and technical innovations) leads to increased energy consumption, which is a typical example of unsustainable behavior. It is important to assess the net effect of efficiency improvements; most empirical investigations show that rebound effects in energy-related domains displace only a small fraction (typically, 10 percent to 30 percent) of the technologically achieved savings. Indeed, rebound effects are closely linked to negative spillover, but entail a different perspective of analysis. The former are analyzed mainly by economists, who suggest that the driving force is represented by price effects so that new technologies increase efficiency and lower prices which in turn allow individuals to spend more in (energy) consumption. The latter, on the other hand, is often interpreted as the outcome of shifts in preferences and motivation, regardless of economic considerations.

Different theories have been proposed to explain negative spillover. Moral licensing (Mazar & Zhong, 2010) represents the phenomenon whereby "when people can call to mind previous instances of their own socially desirable or morally laudable behaviors, they will feel more comfortable taking actions that could be seen as socially undesirable or morally questionable" (Miller & Effron, 2010: 121). In other words, moral licensing has its roots in the observation that moral behaviors, such as those related to sustainability, can be partially explained by how individuals perceive their own moral image. Engaging in responsible behaviors heightens one's own sense of morality, whereas engaging in ethically dubious activities compromises the moral self-image. The consequence is that we tend to behave responsibly when we feel guilty due to a threatened self-image (moral cleansing), while we tend to act less responsibly when we feel our morality strengthened by a recent moral action. The term "licensing" refers to the fact that people, if they perceive they provided their support in an environmental and/or social sensible domain, consider behaving less responsibly in other domains as they have a sort of license deriving from their past behaviors. This is a common psychological mechanism going beyond the borders of sustainable behaviors. It is the case, for instance, of an individual interested in the overall goal of dieting. To achieve her goal, she goes jogging for one hour, burning 700 kcal, and then goes home feeling she had done enough in order to lose weight; as a consequence, she believes it is acceptable to be less rigorous in other aspects related to dieting, ending up eating junk food or a fatty snack.

This is the counterpart of moral cleansing theory (Sachdeva et al., 2009), according to which behaving unsustainably produces guilt which can be alleviated by adopting another responsible behavior. Somewhat related to this is the so-called contribution ethics phenomenon (Guagnano et al., 1994, Kahneman et al., 1993). People feel less obliged to perform tasks in the environmental domain the more they already addressed the same problem by doing something else. The point is that we develop the perception that we cannot solve the whole problem by ourselves, so that once we have done our fair share we feel like we can rest on our laurels and let other actors do their part. Both moral licensing and the contribution ethics phenomena are exacerbated by the tendency of many individuals to exaggerate the real contribution they have provided to the cause (the so-called self-serving bias). This is yet another psychological mechanism that is common in a vast range of contexts. It is, for instance, the case of work groups; typically, all members of the group (whether students working on a group project at college, or employees working in a company) develop the perception that they contributed to the success of the project more than what they actually did.

As anticipated, the consequences of the existence and direction of spillover are extremely relevant, especially for policy-makers. Indeed, as regards sustainability, usually policy-makers have an overarching agenda of protecting the environment in a specific geographical area (which can be either municipal, regional, national, etc.), so that different strategies affecting and targeting specific domains like travel modes, recycling or energy-saving, are indeed different pieces of the same puzzle. If negative spillover holds, this means that strategies aimed at improving sustainability in one domain would just shift the problem elsewhere. For instance, there can be responsible citizens from the standpoint of mobility, but the same citizens can be less environment friendly as regards recycling practices, and so on.

There are also scholars who argue that spillover, either positive or negative, does not exist. Basically they assume that there is no correlation between behaviors whatsoever; behaviors are unique and driven by the specific situation and the individual features of people. Each behavior has its own cluster of predictors so that a general picture of green consumer does not exist. Although the debate is still open and evidence in the literature is not conclusive, it is worth noting that most contributions suggest that spillover actually exists and specifically that it is positive, so that the more I am sustainable in one domain, the more this propagates virtuously to other domains. For a review of both theoretical contributions and empirical investigations, see Lanzini & Thøgersen, 2014, Truelove et al., 2014.

From a practical standpoint, it is important not only to understand if spillover actually occurs, but also the strength of such a phenomenon, and which variables can affect its development the most. If we take for granted, as most of the empirical evidence suggests, that positive spillover occurs across behaviors, we need to understand whether this effect is strong or not, and if there are some behaviors that are more or less affected by spillover itself. What seems to emerge is that most individuals experience a positive spillover across pro-environmental issues as long as the shift towards sustainable behaviors is simple and painless. If it is easy and convenient, both from the standpoint of financial resources and behaviors, to shift from an unsustainable to a sustainable behavior, then spillover is likely to occur. If on the other hand it takes time, cognitive, behavioral and financial resources to change our behaviors, then spillover is not likely to occur.

A methodology to investigate spillover

Now that the relevance of spillover for different stakeholders has been illustrated, it is worth understanding how the phenomenon can be investigated, which are the practical methodologies to assess its existence and strength, as well as some variables that might amplify or reduce its magnitude. Indeed, there are many techniques that can be adopted: the setting can be either a lab experiment or a real-life intervention, the statistical techniques to analyze data might range from regressions to structural equation modeling, and so on. A detailed description of existing methodologies is beyond the scope of the present book; however, Chapter 7 will illustrate a real-life intervention study focusing on spillover and the role exerted by habits and rewards in shaping its trajectories. It suffices here to illustrate a simple yet very effective methodology to investigate the phenomenon, highlighting at once mistakes connected to a dangerous oversimplification that should be avoided. A straightforward approach is to analyze the correlation between behaviors as to obtain a picture of the strength of the connection. Surveys with questions on a set of responsible behaviors are easy to structure. Respondents might be asked (Table 5.1) how often they perform a set of activities,[1] which are the object of the analysis.

Would this be an appropriate way to investigate how the taking up of a virtuous behavior propagates to other behaviors? Maybe not, as correlational studies seem to miss the core of the phenomenon. We are not interested in knowing if, say, an individual that purchases green products also recycles glass in her household; we are interested in knowing if she recycles glass *as a consequence* of purchasing green products. In other words, spillover entails a causal relationship that is overlooked by analyses focusing only on the correlation between different behaviors. An example will clarify the limitations of correlational studies. Let's consider a hypothetical situation where Mark is interviewed on his sustainability-

Table 5.1 Spillover analysis (1)

How often do you perform these activities? (1= never; 7= always)	
Item	*Score*
Commuting by bike	
Commuting by public transport	
Recycling paper	
Recycling glass	
Recycling plastic	
Purchasing organic food	
Purchasing non-food eco-labeled products	
Saving water (turning off water while soaping in the shower)	
Saving electricity (switching off lights when the last person leaving a room)	

related behaviors. When asked how often (on the usual 1 to 7 scale) he purchases eco-labeled products, he answers 6; when asked how often he recycles plastics at home, he answers again 6. What information can be gained from Mark's answers? It emerges that he adopts responsible behaviors as regards both purchasing and recycling. Does this information, on the other hand, provide any useful insight on how one behavior affects the other? What is the effect, in other words, that purchasing green products exerts on recycling activities, or vice versa? Is Mark so careful in recycling as a consequence of his purchasing of green products, or the two activities are not correlated? The answer is that, given the information at hand, it is impossible to know. It could be for instance the case that, since Mark holds strong pro-environmental values, this affects all his behavioral patterns. Or, it could be that while he purchase eco-labeled products because he believes that by doing so he can support the environment, he thinks that recycling has not a relevant impact on sustainability, yet he carries out careful recycling practices only because in his neighborhood waste management taxation is linked to the amount of undifferentiated garbage, so that there is an economic driver behind his activity. More sophisticated techniques are hence needed to investigate in detail the spillover phenomenon, so as to grasp the underpinning mechanisms explaining the relationships between behaviors.

An effective procedure is to set up an intervention that induces the taking up of a virtuous behavior (e.g. purchasing green products) and to observe, after a given period of time, the taking up of other behaviors (e.g. recycling). The intervention has to be implemented so that the overall context does not change and the observed variations in recycling activities can be attributed to the taking up of responsible purchasing behaviors. The same survey on responsible behaviors has to be distributed twice, so that data on participants are collected both before the intervention (to set up the baseline) and after, so as to assess how behaviors changed. In a parallel with the previous example, let's consider Mark's brother, John, being interviewed about his behavioral patterns in sustainability-related domains. An experimental procedure might be organized as follows. First, John is asked how often he performs a given set of such behaviors. Let's imagine that the answers are as in Table 5.2.

At this point, there is a snapshot, a picture of how John behaves in a set of environment-sensitive domains. Since we want to see how different behaviors are interrelated, it is necessary to introduce a change in one of these, and to see how the others change. If, *ceteris paribus,* once John increases his purchases of green products he also improves his recycling, green transportation or resource-saving record, it could be inferred that there has been a positive transmission across behaviors, so that the hypothesis of a positive spillover holds. Clearly, if as a consequence of an increase in green purchases it is observed that John recycles less (or uses less environment-friendly transport modes, and so on), such empirical evidence would be an argument supporting the negative spillover hypothesis. If no variation in recycling or transportation is detected, it might be inferred that behaviors are not correlated, so that spillover does not exist (neither positive, nor negative). Many examples of interventions to trigger the taking up of a virtuous behavior can be imagined. For instance, individuals might be involved in an experiment that proposes that they purchase eco-labeled products for a given period of time, agreeing that they will get a refund for the premium price they have to pay in order to buy environment-friendly goods. Or, to encourage individuals

Table 5.2 Spillover analysis (2)

How often do you perform these activities? (1= never; 7= always)	
Item	*Score*
Choosing a sustainable transport mode	3
Recycling plastic	2
Recycling paper	4
Recycling glass	3
Purchasing non-food eco-labeled products	4
Saving water (turning off water while soaping in the shower)	3
Saving electricity (switching off lights when the last person leaving a room)	3

Table 5.3 Spillover analysis (3)

How often do you perform these activities? (1= never; 7= always)		
Item	*Score time 1*	*Score time 2*
Choosing a sustainable transport mode	3	6
Recycling plastic	2	2
Recycling paper	4	5
Recycling glass	3	2
Purchasing non-food eco-labeled products	4	4
Saving water (turning off water while soaping in the shower)	3	5
Saving electricity (switching off lights when the last person leaving a room)	3	5

to shift from private car use to public transportation, they could be offered a monthly ticket for the bus, and so on. Let's suppose that, in the previous example, after the first survey setting the baseline John is given a free pass to use the public transportation system for three months. Then, once the intervention has ended, the survey asking John to state how often he carries out the same set of behaviors is replicated. So, in Table 5.3, his answers at time 1 (before the intervention) and time 2 (three months later, after the intervention) are reported.

There are more pieces of information compared to the previous example, as it is now possible to see how behavioral patterns evolved during the time-span of the intervention, with John being incentivized to adopt sustainable transport modes by means of free tickets for public transport. As it could be easily predicted, John significantly increased his use of public transportation (6 compared to 3). While this is of little surprise, being a direct consequence of the free tickets, it is more interesting to observe what happened to other behaviors. No relevant changes can be observed as regards recycling (a slight increase in paper recycling and a slight decrease in glass recycling) and green purchasing, while there is a perceptible increase in the adoption of resource-saving activities in the household, as John is more careful in saving electricity and water (from 3 to 5, in both cases). It might be argued that there has been a positive spillover from the transport to the energy-saving domain; as a consequence of the intervention, John indeed improved his record as regards curtailment activities.

However, besides the obvious need to collect and analyze data on a whole sample rather than on a single individual, there is one further step that has to be taken for the experiment to provide accurate and robust evidence on the existence (or the absence) of spillover. It is necessary to analyze the behavior of individuals that did not receive any intervention, to see whether the observed changes are genuinely attributable to spillover, or whether other factors have played a role. This could be the case, for instance, of public authorities implementing an awareness campaign on resource saving in the household during the time span of the experiment. If this is the case, John might have improved his curtailment activities due to the campaign itself rather than to a positive spillover from the travel mode domain. To overcome this limitation, a possible solution is to organize the analysis so that two groups of individuals in the population of interest are interviewed. One group (which is called the *intervention group*) is encouraged to adopt a responsible behavior (for instance, sustainable travel modes by means of free tickets); a second group (the *control group*) does not receive any intervention, so as to observe what is the natural pattern of behavioral development in absence of external manipulations. To complete the relevant taxonomy on spillover, it needs to be specified that the behavior from which the propagation is bound to start (in our example, travel mode) is called the *source behavior*; that is, this behavior is indeed the source of spillover, the behavior from which the phenomenon originates. The other behaviors that might be affected by spillover are called *target behaviors*, as they are the target of the phenomenon we want to investigate. If the two groups significantly differ as regards the taking up of the target behaviors, it means that a positive (or negative) spillover occurred, which is not attributable to external factors other than spillover itself.

In conclusion, this example illustrates a very simplified yet effective methodology to detect spillover across behavioral domains. Although basic compared to other analytical techniques, it represents the bare-bones structure on which more sophisticated research designs can be built. The concluding chapter of the book will indeed present the results of a study on the spillover phenomenon that, although more complex as regards both the experimental design and the analytical techniques, is similar in nature to the present example, of which it represents an integration and a development.

Note

1 This example is purely illustrative. The proposed partition of sustainable behaviors in the domains of modal choice, purchasing, recycling and curtailment is widely adopted in empirical investigations on the topic; yet, there are many other classifications in literature (e.g. Stern, 2000).

References

Abelson, R. P. (1983). Whatever became of consistency theory? *Personality and Social Psychology Bulletin*, 9(1), 37–54.

Bem, D. J. (1972). Self-perception theory. *Advances in Experimental Social Psychology*, 6, 1–62.

Cornelissen, G., Pandelaere, M., Warlop, L., & Dewitte, S. (2008). Positive cueing: Promoting sustainable consumer behavior by cueing common environmental behaviors as environmental. *International Journal of Research in Marketing*, 25(1), 46–55.

Defra, A. (2008). *Framework for Pro-Environmental Behaviours*. London: Department for Environment, Food and Rural Affairs.

Dhar, R., & Simonson, I. (1999). Making complementary choices in consumption episodes: Highlighting versus balancing. *Journal of Marketing Research*, 36(1), 29–44.

Festinger, L. (1957). *A Theory of Cognitive Dissonance*. Evanston, IL: Row Peterson.

Freedman, J. L., & Fraser, S. C. (1966). Compliance without pressure: the foot-in-the-door technique. *Journal of Personality and Social Psychology*, 4(2), 195.

Futerra (2006) *New Rules, New Game: Communications Tactics for Climate Change*, London: Futerra.

Guagnano, G. A., Dietz, T., & Stern, P. C. (1994). Willingness to pay for public goods: A test of the contribution model. *Psychological Science*, 5(6), 411–415.

Hounsham, S. (2006). *Painting the Town Green: How to Persuade People to be Environmentally Friendly: A Report for Everyone Involved in Promoting Greener Lifestyles to the Public*. London: Green-Engage.

Jevons, W. S. *(1865). The Coal Question; An Inquiry Concerning the Progress of the Nation, and the Probable Exhaustion of Our Coal Mines London: Macmillan.*

Kahneman, D., Ritov, I., Jacowitz, K. E., & Grant, P. (1993). Stated willingness to pay for public goods: A psychological perspective. *Psychological Science*, 4(5), 310–315.

Lanzini, P., & Thøgersen, J. (2014). Behavioural spillover in the environmental domain: an intervention study. *Journal of Environmental Psychology*, 40, 381–390.

Mazar, N., & Zhong, C. B. (2010). Do green products make us better people? *Psychological Science*, 21(4), 494–498.

Miller, D. T., & Effron, D. A. (2010). Chapter Three – Psychological License: When it is needed and how it functions. *Advances in Experimental Social Psychology*, 43, 115–155.

Sachdeva, S., Iliev, R., & Medin, D. L. (2009). Sinning saints and saintly sinners: The paradox of moral self-regulation. *Psychological Science*, 20(4), 523–528.

Scott, C. A. (1977). Modifying socially-conscious behavior: The foot-in-the-door technique. *Journal of Consumer Research*, 4(3), 156–164.

Stern, P. C. (2000). New environmental theories: toward a coherent theory of environmentally significant behavior. *Journal of Social Issues*, 56(3), 407–424.

Thøgersen, J., & Crompton, T. (2009). Simple and painless? The limitations of spillover in environmental campaigning. *Journal of Consumer Policy*, 32(2), 141–163.

Truelove, H. B., Carrico, A. R., Weber, E. U., Raimi, K. T., & Vandenbergh, M. P. (2014). Positive and negative spillover of pro-environmental behavior: An integrative review and theoretical framework. *Global Environmental Change*, 29, 127–138.

6 A framework for understanding responsible citizens' behavior

The need for a holistic and flexible approach

The aim of the present volume is not limited to a mere overview of existing theories adopted in the literature to analyze responsible citizens and the determinants of sustainable consumer behavior. Rather, stemming from a systematization of the body of knowledge in the current literature, it represents an attempt to provide a new interpretative framework, capable of supporting scholars and practitioners facing the multi-faceted issue of consumer behavior in sustainability-relevant domains.

It is not by chance that I use the term *interpretative framework* instead of model. Indeed, the genuine added value does not consist of an innovative model marking a difference with existing and validated frameworks. Rather, it provides a framework for practitioners to adopt an evaluation perspective on sustainable behaviors that can be summarized in two words: holistic and flexible. Holistic, as the reader should become familiar with the whole set of behavioral determinants, as set forth by different strands of research. Flexible because, as it has been argued, the role and the salience of different predictors vary with reference to the type of behavior, the context, and subjective features of individuals. Moreover, the same person can act more or less responsibly, according to a set of *factors* that ought to be taken into consideration. There is hence no one-size-fits-all theoretical model that can be used to investigate the topic of interest. Practitioners have to be acquainted and familiar with all the variables shaping behavioral patterns, and have to develop the capability of understanding (given the context and the specific case) which ones are more salient and should be considered.

The present chapter therefore represents the core of the book, as it integrates the main theoretical models with new avenues of research. In this stepwise approach to sustainable behavior analysis, the first step consists of providing the reader with an overview of factors and perspectives that have been so far overlooked by mainstream studies. Some of these (which will be illustrated in detail in the following paragraphs) are not *determinants* of consumer behavior; rather, they are *factors* and *perspectives* that ought to be considered as integrating the set of actual determinants, such as those envisaged by traditional models. It is worth stressing once again that these models represent valid instruments to analyze consumer behavior, and their essential contribution should not by any means be downplayed. On the contrary, their predictive capability proved to be strong over a long period of empirical investigations, and the current chapter does not represent an attempt to provide a new theoretical model in contrast with long-established ones. Rather, it stems from those same models, proposing to the reader a key of interpretation of the complexity of the object of analysis, illustrating the main variables at hand and how some of these can interact one with another.

Before focusing on the factors that have been relegated by mainstream literature on sustainable behavior to ancillary roles, it is worth stressing a first caveat to the reader. By the end of the book, practitioners will go through a broad set of variables and factors that are useful in supporting them in gaining better understandings on what lies behind behavioral patterns of citizens; such knowledge, indeed, represents the prerequisite for effective interventions aimed at shaping courses of action that are consistent with the envisaged objectives.

A first mistake to avoid is to *put everything together*, throwing in all different variables in one single model. A simple addition of variables coming from different strands of research would not provide a useful contribution; on the contrary, practitioners would feel overwhelmed by the plethora of heterogeneous variables, whose combined effect on the behavior of citizens would be excessively complex to be analyzed and understood correctly. Rather, what the reader is to find in this chapter is a sort of interpretation key.

Sustainable behaviors represent, as it has been argued throughout this text, a complex and multifaceted construct. Practitioners can here find guidance, so as to educate themselves on how to single out those elements, perspectives and factors that are relevant and need to be considered on a case-by-case basis. Most theories focus on specific perspectives (in some cases, integrating more than one), yet are not able to grasp the whole complexity of the issue, and to illustrate the entire spectrum of variables that might have a role in determining behavioral trajectories. Moreover, citizens are often considered to hold a certain degree of sustainable responsibility, which is supposed to guide all their behaviors regardless of the context or other contingent factors. In other words, the socio-environmental friendliness of people is considered to be subject to evolution over time, yet in a specific moment is regarded as given, irrespective of the specific situation or domain. If a piece of research identifies that an individual has a high level of environmental friendliness, the traditional approach might suggest that she will act according to this orientation along the whole spectrum of her behavioral patterns. On the other hand, I argue that all of us can be more or less responsible (even given specific attitudes, values, etc.), according to the contextual and psychological situation. Some of these factors affecting our *shade of green* will be presented in the following paragraphs. The sustainability awareness of a person is hence to be considered as a flexible construct, that can vary even within a specific individual according to a set of heterogeneous factors, some of which can be affected from the outside, some of which cannot.

A practitioner dealing with a specific challenge (how to communicate a new product to the market, how to gain an active cooperation of citizens for the implementation of a new policy for recycling in a municipality) does not need to apply a static theory. Again, there is no one-size-fits-all model that can be effective in every scenario and for every individual or community, no framework holding its validity without any regard to some contextual factors, as well as to some variables connected to individuals. The practitioner, in order to shed light on what is sometimes a *black-box* of the determinants of sustainable behaviors, needs to have a) familiarity with all the main variables and behavioral models in the field of sustainability, so as to b) understand which of these are to play a prominent role given the behavior at hand, the specific context and the individuals being investigated. The model has to be flexible and adjusted to the specific object of analysis. Different factors will assume a prominent or a negligible role, according to the specific situation. This book provides practitioners with the theoretical tools to understand how to frame their own analysis, understanding the relationship between the object of analysis and the different strands of research, so as to focus on those specific factors (and interactions) that assume a particular relevance in the specific case.

Factors to be included in the analysis

A common mistake made by both scholars and practitioners is represented by the fact that the analysis is often based on an atomistic approach; a sort of micro-level of analysis that overlooks the required holistic perspective capable of investigating the behavior of individuals also in accordance with the different roles they play in their families, communities or society at large. Caruana and Chatzidakis (2014: 578) state that although "current research privileges only the motivation set of single agents (i.e. the consumer), explanations of CnSR [consumer social responsibility] should usefully consider the influence of various motivations of multiple agents situated at various levels". First of all, it is important to consider the fact that most people are part of a family; as such, their actions can be sometimes affected by the very fact of being "a mother", "a father", "a son", and so on. Most studies do not focus on the effects that being included in a family exert on behaviors, and analyze the behaviors of people as if they would be immanent, irrespective of the "role" they are playing in that moment. Let's clarify this point with an example. Jane, a young woman with two children, has no interest in the sustainability aspects of the food product she purchases. She does not hold strong environmental values, she is not interested in the labor conditions of the workforce occupied along the supply chain of products themselves, and so on. As a consequence, an assessment of this specific individual based on traditional models only is likely to identify Jane as a person that is not interested in the sustainability of an offer based on organic products, and therefore Jane would not be in the target population for commercials and awareness campaigns marketing the product. It is the typical case of so-called "caring consumers", individuals who, given their specific role of parents and the interactions with other members of the family, are spurred into adopting sustainable behaviors from reasons trespassing the boundaries of the self.

The consequences for research are evident, as it does not suffice to focus on an individual adopting an atomistic perspective, without deeper understandings of how she is integrated into a broader network of social and sentimental relations. Moreover, the same individual could act more or less responsibly according to the specific role she is playing in the occasion under scrutiny. Jane might purchase organic food products on a daily basis when the family is all at home; however, Jane herself (the same individual, with the same values, attitudes, awareness) might act differently once she is home alone, as her children are on a one-week holiday with her husband. Focusing on traditional models on consumer behavior is likely to provide the very same results for Jane in both occasions; however, the behavior will differ significantly, so that the predictive capability of models themselves can be strongly hindered by a static approach that does not include the aforementioned role variable. Acknowledging this further factor of complexity, research should avoid dealing with behaviors with a compartmentalized approach. Instead, it should adopt a lens able to provide a broader picture of the individual, who has to be analyzed in connection with the groups and community she is part of, and the mutual relationships with other individuals.

As we are part of groups and networks other than those relating to family ties, it is important to focus also on these, so as to improve our understanding on how responsible behavioral patterns are affected by the social environment we are part of. For instance, we can stick to the example of Jane. Not only she is a mother, and it has been illustrated how this role might have an impact on her behaviors (specifically, on her decisions regarding purchasing of food products). Jane also works and her role in the workplace (and the network of social interactions it entails) represent yet a further dimension to be considered. Some scholars label this phenomenon as the *work–life balance spillover*, acknowledging the mutual influences between the private sphere and the working life: "work and non-work roles might influence one another, building on psychological constructs such as affect, cognition and values" (Singh & Bhatnagar, 2015: 309). Whereas the main concept of behavioral spillover has been previously discussed in Chapter 5, it here suffices to stress how the interaction between the working and the private dimension of individuals' lives can bear both beneficial and detrimental effects from the standpoint of sustainable behaviors. For instance, an employee involved in sustainability-related activities on the workplace might be spurred on to act similarly at home (being this a typical instance of positive spillover). However, spillover could be also negative, thanks to a compensatory effect exerting a negative influence as we perceive *we have done our fair share* at work. As a consequence, a sort of contribution ethics effect might arise, making us less attentive to sustainability-related considerations. The first suggestion to shed light on the mechanisms underpinning responsible behaviors is hence the necessity to consider an individual not as a static agent who behaves according to predefined rules in every situation of her everyday life. On the contrary, all the roles she plays as a worker, a consumer, a member of family and social networks (as well as the intertwining effects that such roles imply) need to be considered.

A second aspect linked to the oversimplification which sometimes affects analyses on sustainable behaviors is reflected in the frequent overlooking of links between given variables (like, for instance, age or gender, or even psychographics) and the different theoretical components of environmental consciousness. Indeed, this can be disentangled in factors such as knowledge about sustainability issues, attitudes, and actual behaviors. Attempts at profiling individuals with no reference to all three dimensions miss the broad picture, providing only a partial and inaccurate snapshot. Let's consider, for instance, how a person who is aware of sustainability issues will not automatically develop positive attitudes driving future behaviors. There is robust evidence corroborating this assumption, as "the empirical evidence for this relationship [between knowledge and behavior] is far from clear" (Johnstone & Tan, 2015: 313). Hines and colleagues (1987) conducted a meta-analysis finding the correlation between environmental knowledge and behaviors to be small; it can be speculated that individuals do not always act based on rational cognitive processes, and their actual behaviors are also heavily affected by intuitive and emotional factors (Chan,

2001). Not only does the literature highlight a gap between knowledge and behavior; the attitude–behavior gap refers to the phenomenon and the impeding factors according to which even people with positive attitudes towards sustainability often do not act consistently (Chatzidakis et al., 2004). Let's consider, for instance, purchasing activities and the frequent occurrence of "consumers' positive attitudes about the environment [that] do not necessarily translate into actual purchase behavior" (Johnstone & Tan, 2015: 313).

Inner motivations are at the base of the adoption of sustainable behaviors, yet they are often overlooked by mainstream research. This is relevant, since not only specific features of individuals need to be analyzed, but also the relative intensity of underlying motivations that are diverse in nature. Caruana and Chatzidakis (2014: 580) state that "fundamental human needs provide a motivational context for agents to engage in responsibility". The motivations driving sustainable behaviors can be ascribed to three categories: moral, instrumental, and relational. Furthermore, they can also vary with respect to the level of analysis (whether we focus on a single agent or, for instance, on a member of a social group). It can be argued, therefore, that an adequate understanding of responsible behaviors should be based on a multi-agent, multi-level approach.

Moral motivations can be considered as the purest driver of behaviors, as they stem from an altruistic concern for others, which can be individuals but can also be the natural environment. Such motivations are the object of analysis of most research on responsible citizens. Instrumental motivations, on the other hand, pertain expectations of individuals to *get something out of* their behaviors. Typical examples are represented by people who buy organic products driven by the desire to receive health benefits, or even the thrill of enjoyment-related experience, like the chance to visit organic farms.

Third, relational motivations address the need of individuals to care for peers, family or members of social networks, and to comply with norms that shape relations with others. This becomes particularly salient in the domain of sustainability, as many behaviors are performed in presence of others (or keeping others in mind); people choose to act responsibly as a way of satisfying relational needs. In line with the holistic approach – which represents the guiding light of this contribution – it is important to stress how studies of responsible citizens should focus on all three dimensions, as people are spurred to action by different motivations. The salience of each type of motivation may vary on a case-by-case basis, given both subjective factors and the specific behavior and context at hand. This might look trivial, however, most traditional frameworks (including those illustrated in Chapter 2) focus only on one specific set of motivations. They hence ignore the overarching perspective that represents an essential ingredient for a sound investigation of the true motives underpinning responsible behaviors. If we consider the work of Ajzen and Fishbein and their theories of reasoned action (Ajzen & Fishbein, 1980; Fishbein & Ajzen, 1975) and planned behavior (Ajzen, 1991), we notice that the focus is on attitudes and norms; these represent, to some extent, constructs similar to instrumental and relational motives respectively. Moral motives appear to be out of the picture, while they represent the cornerstone of yet another popular strand of research on sustainable behaviors: Schwartz's work and his norm-activation model which focuses on personal norms and values, and which displays an evident overlap with moral motives.

Another factor that is often overlooked by mainstream research is represented by a specific focus on how individuals process anticipated costs and benefits of the activity at hand (Freestone & McGoldrick, 2008), and how such an evaluation is affected by the stage of awareness that people experience: simple awareness, concern and then action (Miller & Rollnick, 2003). Let's consider, for instance, a person that may be considering carrying out careful recycling activities in her household. This behavior entails a trade-off between the benefits deriving from such course of action, and the costs which it entails. Among the benefits we can mention, for instance, financial advantages (in case the garbage fee is connected to the amount of unsorted waste produced) or the pleasure that derives from feelings of supporting a right cause, such as that of preserving the environment by means of daily activities. On the other hand, there are costs associated with careful recycling activities, such as the time (and sometimes effort) spent in sorting out garbage, or the need to collect information on how to effectively carry out the recycling of household waste. Individuals who adopt a rational process of evaluation of trade-offs will choose the proposed alternative in cases where benefits outweigh costs, and vice versa. However, it is not irrelevant to know whether the individual is experiencing early stages of generic awareness about recycling activities and their impacts on sustainability ("I know"), actual concern for the topic ("I care") or predisposition for action ("I do"). Typically (though not always) individuals in early stages of ethical awareness tend to focus predominantly on the negative aspects of the behavior at hand, underestimating feelings of the beneficial impacts of the latter both for them and for environment/society at large. In the previous example, the individual will be worried about the extra effort and the "waste" of time that performing careful recycling activities would entail, with little consideration for the aforementioned positive aspects.

However, as people increase environmental awareness and *move up the ladder* towards the concern and, eventually, action stages, the salience of positive aspects associated with sustainable behaviors increases, outperforming the relevance of cost-related aspects.

The consequence for scholars investigating the determinants of sustainable behaviors (and agents interested in shaping them) is that it is worth understanding where people stand on such a path. In other words, a dynamic perspective is needed, as the same result can imply different prospects for future behaviors, according to whether an individual is aware of the sustainability issue, concerned about it or already ready for action. For instance, if traditional studies conclude that a person has "mild" positive attitudes towards purchasing a green product, there is a big difference whether the same person is in the early stages of awareness (hence showing great room for improvement) or whether is a mature consumer from the standpoint of sustainability, so that it is not likely that in the future the concern and the willingness to take action will increase significantly.

Before proceeding with the proposition of an interpretative framework supporting practitioners in analyzing responsible citizens and the determinants of sustainable behaviors, it is worth to devote a few lines to summarize the evidence emerging from the overview on existing models on behavior as presented in Chapter 2 and integrated in earlier paragraphs of this chapter. The most severe limitation is represented by an over-simplification of a complex, multi-dimensional construct. Most research stems from a specific theoretical framework, considered as the best option irrespective of the specific empirical setting at hand. For instance, it might be assumed that the theory of planned behavior is the most effective predictive model in the field of sustainability, so that its application can be "copied and pasted" in every domain and context of interest. On the other hand, I argue that there is no such *best theory*, as there are many factors (stemming from different theories and strands of research) that might play a prominent role in the specific case of interest. Existing theories should not be taken as monoliths with a fideistic approach. It is the educated practitioner who should understand which bricks from which framework should be considered for every specific analysis that is to be performed, or else results would reflect only *part of the story*, missing a holistic approach required by the articulation of the construct. Furthermore, a relational perspective (Tencati & Zsolnai, 2012) should be added to the traditional view of individuals as single, atomistic agents. In consumer behavior (and especially in the case of sustainability) social expectations, family and community ties do play a crucial role in shaping the course of action. Interpretation of sustainable behaviors should, in conclusion, be based on a contingency-based, multi-level interpretation going beyond the boundaries of a simplistic and partial modeling.

The proposition of an innovative interpretative framework

The interpretative framework I propose stems from the acknowledgement, on the one hand, of the validity of current models in detecting the main determinants of sustainable behaviors and, on the other hand, the necessity of breaking free from a simplistic interpretation of such behaviors and the mechanisms that shape them, recognizing that the complexity and multi-dimensionality of the construct requires a holistic view based on a multi-level, flexible approach. The reader should be familiar with the different strands of research and theoretical models. Each model focuses on a precise set of predictors of behavior: the theory of planned behavior, for instance, assumes that behaviors stem from a rational cognitive process where behavioral intentions (the closest predictor of behaviors) are shaped by attitudes, norms and behavioral control. Similarly, the norm-activation model focuses on feelings of moral obligation rooted in the awareness of consequences of given behaviors on the environment and society at large and on ascription of responsibility for such detrimental impacts, and so on. Indeed, practitioners should develop the capability to *read* the specific situation at hand, understanding its specificities and which factors and variables are likely to play a prominent role. In other words, I argue that it is a fruitless exercise to compare different models so as to rank them with respect to their predictive capability and effectiveness in detecting the determinants of sustainable behaviors. All models focus on a specific set of variables. As such, they only get part of the picture. At the same time, behaviors are so different one from another that I believe there is no *one-size-fits-all* model capable of explaining better than others the mechanisms underpinning the development of given courses of action. In some cases planned behavior framework might represent the best option, whereas in other situations, characterized by the salience of environmental values and the relevant consequences of misconduct (and feelings of personal responsibility that follow), the norm-activation model might have a higher explanatory potential. Likewise, there are cases where a combination of different models should be adopted, with the integration of the basic structure of a specific theoretical model with elements that are typical of other streams of research. Moreover, it is worth stressing once again that the sustainability level of a person should not be considered as given, as the same individual can act more or less sustainably when the context, the role, the contingencies of the situation vary. When it comes to sustainability and responsible behaviors, not only we all come in different colors: we come in different shades of green, and the shade itself can vary, even significantly, not only between persons but also as far as the same individual is concerned.

Whereas flexibility is the key concept, in this volume I propose an overarching interpretative framework to provide the broad structure under which practitioners can work as to frame the specific analytical strategy to assess the behaviors and the situations at hand.

First of all, I argue that there are two levels of analysis. On the one hand, there are what can be defined as proper determinants (or predictors) of sustainable behaviors. These predictors are the building blocks of the theoretical models that have been illustrated in the dedicated chapter of this book: attitudes, norms, habits, values, and so on. On the other hand, there are *factors*, which cannot be considered as predictors of behavior *per se*. Rather, they represent variables and perspectives that need to be considered in synergy with behavioral determinants, so as to shed light on how these develop. It is the case, for instance, of the effect exerted by factors such as social roles individuals play (within families, at work, and so on), the cross-fertilization across behaviors by means of spillover effects, and so on.

The interpretative framework I propose is based on a funnel-like representation of determinants and factors shaping sustainable behaviors. First and foremost, I argue that these are the result of the integration of rational cognitive processes and automatic responses to goal-oriented cues (Layer 1). Consistent with most literature on the topic (and with a simplification made necessary by the need to synthesize complex constructs in a single term), I will label these two components as intentions and habits, respectively. There is no hierarchy between these two broad categories of determinants: we cannot say that, in general, habits are more relevant in predicting sustainable behaviors than intentions, or vice versa. There are clearly some factors the reader is by now familiar with that support or hinder the salience of one component over the other. For instance, the stability of the external context is a typical instance of factors triggering the prominence of automatic responses and the role of habits in shaping behavioral patterns. It is the practitioner that, with a *case-by-case* approach, should evaluate which of the two dimensions plays a prominent role, and to which extent. A second level is represented by three categories of behavioral determinants that refer to the individual, relational and contextual sphere, respectively (Layer 2).

Behavioral predictors of the individual sphere are those that are more closely related to subjective features of the individual. It is the case, for instance, of attitudes and values. As such, in other words, they pertain to the *self*. The relational sphere pertains, on the other hand, to predictors that gain strength from the fact that individuals are inserted in a multi-level network of social relations: people are part of communities and social groups, and the relationship with other subjects bears the potential of affecting own behaviors. Let's consider, for instance, the case of subjective norms. These reflect social pressure, as they deal with the effect that the judgment of our peers has on us carrying out a specific activity. In parallel with individual determinants, we can state that relational determinants pertain to the *others*. The contextual sphere refers to those variables dealing with the broader context in which behavioral intentions and habits develop, shaping future courses of action. As such, they do not pertain either to the subjective sphere of the individual, or to the community she is part of. Some of the contextual variables might refer, for instance, to the behavior itself, which might be intrinsically easy or difficult to perform. The specific example of task complexity is also useful to illustrate how some variables can affect more than one category. For instance, intrinsic and objective task complexity is a contextual variable. At the same time, however, it has a clear overlap with determinants that pertain to the individual sphere, such as perceived behavioral control, and how difficult we *perceive* an activity is to be carried out. In a parallel with the previous dimensions, we can say that contextual variables pertain, indeed, to the *context*.

On top of the funnel structure, there are some factors that need to be considered (Layer 3), as they *filter* important perspectives, determining which of the blocks at the lower level (pertaining to the self, to others and to the context) play a prominent role in the specific case, and providing new keys of interpretation that should be considered in the analysis. These factors have been illustrated in previous sections of this chapter and pertain, for instance, to the need to analyze individuals with reference to the link between specific predictors and all the components of responsible consciousness (knowledge, attitudes and actual behaviors), to the mechanisms adopted by citizens to process anticipated costs and benefits of a specific behavior, and so on.

Figure 6.1 synthesizes the funnel approach: the arrows indicate that every dimension in Layer 2 (individual, relational and contextual sphere) can exert an influence on both intentions and habits. For instance, if we focus on the individual sphere, beliefs, attitudes and values are typical antecedents of behavioral intentions, while other subjective traits of personality such as the resistance to change investigated by the Oreg scale (Oreg, 2003) affect how prone are individuals towards developing habits. And the same can apply to the relational and contextual spheres, as well.

The proposed approach might resemble the structure of traditional models on consumer behavior. Indeed, it shows intentions and habits as the closest antecedents of behavior, and these being affected by a set of determinants referring to both subjective and non-subjective dimensions. As such, one could speculate that it represents a sort of development of the planned behavior framework, or a modified version of Triandis's theory

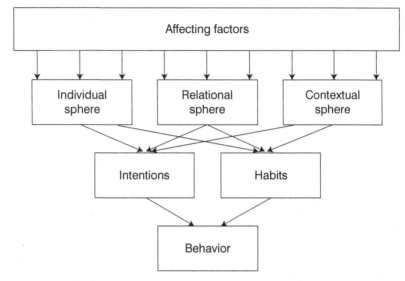

Figure 6.1 The funnel approach

of interpersonal behavior. Likewise, similarities could be detected also with respect to other popular frameworks widely adopted in empirical investigations on consumer behavior in sustainability-related domains.

However, there are some defining features that differentiate the funnel perspective from existing models, though these represent the building blocks on which the former can be based. These defining features reflect, for instance, the need to consider upstream affecting factors that affect how different determinants of sustainable behaviors interact in shaping intentions and in building habits. Even more so, a novel aspect is represented by the flexibility in considering specific determinants (stemming from heterogeneous theoretical frameworks) according to the contingencies of the specific situation. Let's consider, for instance, two different sustainable behaviors: green volunteering and curtailment behaviors such as turning off lights when being the last person to leave a room. These two behaviors represent typical instances of sustainable behaviors (Thøgersen & Ölander, 2003). A traditional approach would state that there is a specific theoretical model that is better able to explain responsible behaviors, regardless of their specificities. If such an assumption holds, it means that a given theoretical framework (planned behavior, value–belief–norms, habits, norm-activation, or others) would be the most effective in predicting both curtailment behaviors and volunteering activities. I argue that this is not the case, as the specifics of the object of the analysis (both the agent and the behavior) make some determinants more salient over others, so that, once again, there is no one-size-fits-all model outperforming others in predicting all sustainable behaviors. In our example, for instance, some elements might be salient in the curtailment behavior (e.g. stability of the context triggering the development of habits) but not in activism; on the contrary, values are likely to be a prominent factor in volunteering, yet play a marginal role in curtailment behaviors. Furthermore, the relational sphere is likely to be a relevant factor in volunteering (both for the willingness to provide a concrete help to the community, and for the social image that gets strengthened by such activities), while economic considerations might play a role in affecting curtailment behaviors in the household (due to the lower bills derived from saving energy), and so on.

In conclusion, the new interpretative approach that I propose should be considered as an integration, rather than a dismissal, of current models investigating behaviors in the field of sustainability. It represents an attempt to build bridges between different strands of research, advocating a flexible approach where factors stemming from different models can be integrated in one overarching framework. Far from suggesting a simple summation of different theories – with the consequent explosion of variables to be considered that would lead to a hard-to-handle over-complexity – the proposed approach is based on the assumption that educated practitioners should recognize the specifics of the object of analysis (in terms of specific behavior, individuals, contextual variables, and so on), and focus on those determinants that are likely to play a prominent role, on a case-by-case basis. The interpretative framework should be structured so as to follow three subsequent layers of analysis: first, specific factors that are often overlooked in current research, yet bear the potential of heavily affecting the accuracy of subsequent analyses (Layer 3); second, categories of behavioral determinants that refer to three different spheres – the self, the others and the context (Layer 2); third, the acknowledgement that both rational cognitive processes and automatic responses to familiar situations interact in shaping behavioral patterns, with the specific case determining the prominence of one dimension over the other (Layer 1). Investigating responsible citizens and the determinants of sustainable behaviors represents a complex task, requiring adequate knowledge of different theoretical frameworks and high analytical skills so as to interpret the specific features of the behavior at hand. Yet, this represents the price to be paid to gain deep understanding of a phenomenon that is by its nature complex and multi-faceted, an over-simplification of which probably represented the main reason for the heterogeneous results affecting existing research, and the subsequent effectiveness in supporting decision processes of businesses and policy-makers. The task is demanding, yet the prize is well worth the effort.

References

Ajzen, I. (1991). The theory of planned behavior. *Organizational Behavior and Human Decision Processes*, 50(2), 179–211.

Ajzen, I., & Fishbein, M. (1980). *Understanding Attitudes and Predicting Social Behaviour.* Englewood Cliffs, NJ: Prentice-Hall.

Caruana, R., & Chatzidakis, A. (2014). Consumer social responsibility (CnSR): Toward a multi-level, multi-agent conceptualization of the "other CSR". *Journal of Business Ethics*, 121(4), 577–592.

Chan, R. Y. (2001). Determinants of Chinese consumers' green purchase behavior. *Psychology & Marketing*, 18(4), 389–413.

Chatzidakis, A., Hibbert, S., Mittusis, D., & Smith, A. (2004). Virtue in consumption? *Journal of Marketing Management*, 20(5–6), 526–543.

Fishbein, M., & Ajzen, I. (1975). *Belief, Attitude, Intention and Behavior: An Introduction to Theory and Research.* Reading, MA: Addison-Wesley.

Freestone, O. M., & McGoldrick, P. J. (2008). Motivations of the ethical consumer. *Journal of Business Ethics*, 79(4), 445–467.

Hines, J. M., Hungerford, H. R., & Tomera, A. N. (1987). Analysis and synthesis of research on responsible environmental behavior: A meta-analysis. *The Journal of Environmental Education*, 18(2), 1–8.

Johnstone, M. L., & Tan, L. P. (2015). Exploring the gap between consumers' green rhetoric and purchasing behaviour. *Journal of Business Ethics*, 132(2), 311–328.

Miller, W., & Rollnick, S. (2003). Motivational interviewing: Preparing people for change. *Journal for Healthcare Quality*, 25(3), 46.

Oreg, S. (2003). Resistance to change: developing an individual differences measure. *Journal of Applied Psychology*, 88(4), 680.

Singh, H., & Bhatnagar, J. (2015). Green work-life balance. In S. Chatterjee, N.P. Singh, D.P. Goyal, & N. Gupta (eds) *Managing in Recovering Markets* (pp. 303–313). New Delhi: Springer.

Tencati, A., & Zsolnai, L. (2012). Collaborative enterprise and sustainability: The case of slow food. *Journal of Business Ethics*, 110(3), 345–354.

Thøgersen, J., & Ölander, F. (2003). Spillover of environment-friendly consumer behaviour. *Journal of Environmental Psychology*, 23(3), 225–236.

7 From theory to practice
A real-life intervention study

Investigating sustainable behaviors: an intervention study

The reader has been guided on a long journey through the domain of responsible citizens and sustainable consumer behaviors, which shed light both on theoretical frameworks broadly adopted in the existing literature, and on avenues for future research stemming from the acknowledgment of those gaps that still need to be addressed in studies to come. The research agenda is full and challenging, as deeper understanding of the topic requires new perspectives of analysis and a renewed attention on specific variables, some of which have been described in detail in previous chapters. To support this demanding task with a sound approach, a new interpretative framework has been proposed providing practitioners with conceptual and methodological guidelines to be adopted in the study of complex and multi-faceted constructs, such as those at hand.

To this point, the book has displayed a clear (and necessary) theoretical orientation; in this sense the present chapter provides a useful integration to *complete the circle*, as it illustrates in detail how to transfer the theoretical considerations set forth previously into practical research, hence representing a sort of empirical appendix to the book.

Empirical investigations on sustainable behaviors represent a *mare magnum* where different methodological approaches and statistical techniques coexist. The former can range, for instance, from ethnographic studies to lab-set experiments, or from large-scale real-life intervention studies to simple focus groups, and so on. Similarly, the latter can range from qualitative to quantitative techniques, from simple regression analyses to more complex structural equation modeling techniques, and so on. Acknowledging the heterogeneity that characterizes studies on the topic, I choose to focus on a Denmark-based study which I conducted in the field of sustainable behavior, as I deem it particularly fit for the purpose. Indeed, it represents one of the few existing studies focusing synergically on most of the constructs at the base of previous discussions (including, among others, key aspects such as habits, incentives and spillover) and it represents a rare example of research where specific phenomena (e.g. habit–spillover or incentive–spillover relationships) are investigated with real-life interventions rather than in lab settings. The project was conducted in the framework of my doctoral thesis, and some results have been published in a 2014 article focusing on pro-environmental spillover (Lanzini & Thøgersen, 2014). Although sophisticated statistical techniques are used in the article, I here prefer to illustrate a simple methodology using basic statistics, so as to prove that when the design is sound, even extremely simple statistical calculations allow obtaining interesting and insightful results.

The focus of the project is sustainable consumer behavior and, more specifically, how behaviors in different domains are interrelated. The reader is by now familiar with the concept of spillover; it therefore suffices to add that the study investigates not only the existence itself of (positive or negative) spillover, but also whether (and how) elements such as habits and incentives affect the development of spillover trajectories. That is, I might be interested in investigating whether spillover is more likely to be triggered if the target behavior is performed habitually by individuals, or vice versa. Or, I might be wishing to analyze if encouraging individuals to perform a sustainable behavior by means of monetary, rather than non-monetary, rewards does make a difference both with respect to the direct impact on the behavior that is the object of the inducement, and to broader behavioral patterns.

Conceptually, the project can therefore be reduced to two consecutive steps. The first step is aimed at determining whether spillover exists, so that the adoption of a pro-environmental behavior leads to changes also in other, unrelated domains. To this end, the project addresses a first, overarching research question that can be formulated as follows:

> *RQ1: Does acting pro-environmentally in a behavioral domain have a positive impact (i.e. positive spillover) on other, non-correlated behavioral domains?*

It should be stressed at the outset that a novel aspect of the research consists in the fact that it goes beyond a mere assessment of the existence (and, eventually, the strength) of spillover across behaviors, investigating instead the mediating role that variables like habits or incentives (monetary and not) have on spillover itself. Consistently with this, in case of evidence corroborating the existence of spillover (RQ1), the second step of the project analyzes the role that such variables play in affecting spillover trajectories, addressing the following research questions:

RQ2: Is pro-environmental spillover affected by the type of incentives (monetary or praise rewards) adopted to support the source behavior?

RQ3: Is spillover from one (source) to another (target) pro-environmental behavior stronger in individuals that already habitually perform the target behavior, compared to individuals with less habitual target behavior?

Methods

To answer the research questions of the project, I designed a panel study consisting of two waves of surveys, distributed online and administered before and after an experimental intervention. Intervention (or experimental) study designs are characterized by the fact that researchers deploy a certain type of intervention at some point throughout the study. So, typically, the researcher assesses (through simple observation, measurement, surveys, and so on) a specific object of analysis (a phenomenon, a behavior, etc.) both before and after the intervention is implemented, so as to determine if the latter had any impact. Since the phenomenon to be investigated is the spillover effect, and the empirical setting is that of sustainable behaviors, an apt intervention might consist in encouraging individuals to perform a given pro-environmental behavior more often than usual (or, make them take up a new pro-environmental behavior). Accordingly, in my project I incentivize green purchasing, as will be described shortly.

The convenience sample of the study is composed of 194 undergraduate students from the University of Aarhus, Denmark. This represents a limitation of the study, since student-based samples are sometimes criticized for not being representative of the overall population, as individuals come from one single age group and share specific features that hinder the generalizability of results.

Students were contacted by email and asked if they were willing to participate in a study on consumer behavior, which might imply the purchase of specific *green* products for a limited period of time. Box 7.1 presents the recruiting message that was distributed to students.

Students participating in the study received by email the first questionnaire[1] (see Appendix to this chapter), which had been formulated in English, and then translated in Danish.[2] Both versions have been pretested on a sample of 10 students as to check the clarity of the questions and whether these could lead to misunderstanding or multiple interpretations. Moreover, the Danish questionnaire had been back-translated into English, as to avoid translation shortcomings related to poor conceptual or cultural correspondence of the two texts.

Box 7.1 The recruitment message

Dear student

We are recruiting participants for a study on consumer behavior.

Students participating in the study will have the chance to *win different interesting prizes* by means of a final lottery draw.

You can enroll by sending an email to [...], with the subject "Consumer Behavior Study".

Participants, once enrolled, will receive specific instructions via email. The tasks are limited to filling two brief questionnaires online, and to keep track for a period of few weeks of their purchasing patterns with respect to a given list of product categories (e.g. milk, fruit). This will be done by means of a shopping diary to be filled in (very simple, should take around one minute per shopping occasion).

The questionnaire begins with some introductory questions on demographics and general background, including an assessment of acceptance of both *green taxes* and policies restricting consumer behaviors in environment-sensitive domains. Moreover, involvement/concern for environmental issues is investigated through the revised New Ecological Paradigm Index (Dunlap et al., 2000).

The questionnaire is then divided into three main sections, focusing respectively on behavioral intentions, pro-environmental behaviors, and habits. In the first section, respondents are presented with a battery of 17 pro-environmental behaviors and asked to answer for each one of them to the question "*How likely do you think you will do [X] in the next occasion, if you have the chance to do so?*" (where [X] stands for each behavior), adopting a seven-point scale ranging from *very unlikely* to *very likely*.

In the second section on pro-environmental behaviors, respondents are asked to state how often they perform each of the previously mentioned behaviors. Behavioral patterns are measured by questions of the "*How often do you [X]*" type, with [X] referring to each green behavior. The answers are on a seven-point scale, labeled *never, very rarely, rarely, half the time, often, very often* and *always*. The basis for the selection of relevant environmental behaviors was a study commissioned by the Danish Environment and Consumer Agencies (Forbrugerstyrelsen og Miljøstyrelsen, 1996), already adopted as the framework for the environmental impact of consumption in other researches on spillover (see Thøgersen & Ölander, 2003). However, the list has been modified to better fit the specifics of the study, encompassing the inclusion of further pro-environmental behaviors and the removal of others. The broad behavioral categories considered are purchasing, transport mode, energy/resources conservation, and recycling.

The third section is devoted to resistance to change and habitudinal patterns. Resistance to change is investigated adopting the Oreg Scale (2003), designed to measure dispositional inclination to resist change by focusing on factors like routine seeking, cognitive rigidity, reaction to imposed change and short-term focus. Habits on the other hand are investigated relying on the Self-Reported Habit Index (Verplanken & Orbell, 2003).

Once the data were collected, the resulting *snapshot* shed light on the status quo before manipulations and experimental interventions were deployed, providing a basis for inter-temporal comparison allowing the singling out of eventual spillover effects and the impact of both habit strength and different types of rewards (monetary vs praise).

After the completion of the first wave of questionnaires, the sample has been randomly divided into three groups: one *control* group and two *experimental-intervention* groups (*monetary* and *praise*). The control group received no intervention, and has been analyzed so as to control for possible evolutions in the behaviors of participants not ascribable to experimental interventions. A typical example could be an eventual change in choice of transport mode, driven by a change in season and weather conditions between the two waves of surveys.

The monetary and praise group members were respectively treated with monetary and praise rewards. The former were compensated for the expenditure they had to bear in order to purchase green products (which typically entail a premium price) and participated in a lottery draw with monetary prizes. The latter, on the other hand, received no monetary inducement, but only appraisal messages thanking them for their cooperation and stressing the contribution they provided to a good cause. Participants in the intervention groups received instructions by email on how to proceed with the experiment. Boxes 7.2 and 7.3 present the message sent to members of both groups, and the shopping diary with relevant instructions. Whereas the first part of the text was common for all participants, the second part was different for students in the monetary and in the praise conditions.

At this point, monetary and praise group members were encouraged to buy organic food and other eco-labeled products for a period of six weeks. The choice of the source behavior which was supported with incentives was driven by the fact that it represented a behavior where there is money involved and the need to bear extra costs such as the premium price required for the purchase of such products. Participants have been also asked to record in a shopping diary their purchases in a set of product categories, specifying whether they opted for an environmentally friendly version (e.g. organic milk

Box 7.2 **Instructions message**

Dear participant, as part of the experiment we encourage you to consider environment-friendly alternatives when shopping in the next six weeks. You will be asked to print out and keep updated the shopping diary attached to the present email (containing instructions for its correct compilation, as well). As to have the chance to process more data, we ask you to keep the receipts of your purchases with the diary (do not worry if some receipts will be missing, yet please try to collect as many as possible). We wish to stress that <u>all gathered information is strictly confidential</u>, and each student-id will be matched with an anonymous alphanumeric code to ensure privacy and the absence of any link between the shopping diary and the generalities of the participant. At the end of the 6-weeks period, you will be asked to hand in the shopping diary and the receipts (the specific date and venue will be communicated to you by email in the following weeks).

(<u>Monetary group only</u>) On this occasion, you will receive a monetary compensation for the premium price you had to sustain in order to purchase environment-friendly products. Moreover, you will participate in a lottery draw among experiment participants, with prizes consisting of 2,000 DKK.[3]

(<u>Praise group only</u>) – Last but not least, the research team wants to take the opportunity for a personal note, and to thank you for your participation in the project. We believe that sustainable purchasing and consumption patterns are a very important topic in the research field of sustainability, as it is necessary to shift current behavioral trends into a more sustainable paradigm. Your participation in the project contributes on building knowledge that will in turn be useful to develop specific and effective policies addressing this environmental issue.

vs traditional milk, etc). Receipts had to be kept to allow cross-checking at the end of the experiment, as participants failing to show such proof of purchase were assumed not to have complied with the requirements of the experiment, and were subsequently dropped from the sample to be analyzed.

Both monetary rewards and mailing services covered a six-week period, and contacts with members of the two groups have been in equal number and frequency. Such contacts consisted of *follow-up* emails, that had the goal of reviving the salience of monetary vs praise messages. Box 7.4 illustrates an example of such messages for both groups.

Box 7.3 Shopping diary

During the six weeks of the experiment, you are asked to record in the table "Shopping Diary" (see below) every single purchase of products belonging to one of the following categories:

– Food products (milk; yoghurt; eggs; meat; vegetables; fruit)

– Non-food products (detergents for the house; soaps, shampoos and other products for personal hygiene; kitchen paper; toilet paper)

Please use one line[4] for each product purchased, and fill in the table as instructed below:

Column 1: "Purchase episode". Simply tick with an X every time you purchase a product of the category (each time on a different line)

Column 2: "Date of purchase". For each product, please record the date of purchase (day/month).

Column 3: "Green option?" FUNDAMENTAL!! For each product purchased, please tick this box with an X if the product itself represents an *environment-friendly* alternative, or leave the box blank if it represents a *traditional* product. By environment-friendly alternative we consider products with an organic food label (in the case of food products), or products with eco-labels like the EU Flower, or equivalent (in the case of non-food products).

Product category	Purchase episode	Date of purchase	Green option?
Milk			
Yoghurt			
Eggs			
Meat			
Vegetables			
Fruit			
Detergents for the house			
Soaps and shampoos			
Kitchen paper			
Toilet paper			

> **Box 7.4 Reminder emails**
>
> *Monetary group*
> Dear participant, you have by now completed the first two weeks of the experiment on consumer behavior. The experiment will last four more weeks. At the end, you will be asked to hand in your shopping diary along with the receipts at [...]
>
> On that occasion, you will receive a *monetary compensation* for your green purchases, whereas the final lottery draw (where you will have the *chance to win 2,000DKK*) will take place at the end of the project.
>
> *Praise group*
> Dear participant, you have by now completed the first two weeks of the experiment on consumer behavior. The experiment will last four more weeks.
>
> We remind you that at the end of the experiment you will be asked to hand in your shopping diary along with the receipts at [...].
>
> The research team takes the opportunity to thank you for participating in the experiment, and is glad to send in attachment some information on the benefits for the common good and the environment that derive from purchasing organic food and eco-labeled products.
>
> All of us, as citizens of this planet, have to do our part.
> *Thank you for doing yours...*

Once the six weeks timeframe had elapsed, a second questionnaire, an exact replication of the first, was circulated to gain insights on the effects of the different stimulae on behaviors and the spillover between them. Comparison with the control group allowed controlling for modifications of individuals' behavioral patterns not induced by the interventions. Incentives were at this point terminated and both praise and monetary group members were debriefed, thanking them for the participation in the study and informing them that they might have been contacted in the upcoming weeks for some follow-up questions.

Results

A first glimpse at the results suggests that students in the experimental condition – who had been induced to purchase green products – at the end of the project were also more willing to act consistently in other domains, compared with students in the control condition: more willing to save water and energy in the household, to choose eco-friendly transport modes, and so on.[5, 6] In other words, preliminary data analysis seemingly suggests the existence of a positive spillover across behaviors. A simple yet effective statistical technique to test the robustness of such findings is represented by analysis of variance (ANOVA), which represents a family of statistical methods based on the testing of differences between means. In particular, I conducted a one-way between-groups analysis of covariance (ANCOVA) so as to analyze differences in the scores of groups (the post-intervention scores on behavioral intentions for students in the experimental and in the control group) while controlling for an additional continuous variable as covariate (the pre-intervention scores on behavioral intentions).

Table 7.1 shows that there are significant differences between the experimental and the control groups for different items such as turning off water while soaping in the shower ($F = 7.747$, $p<.01$, partial $\eta^2 = .039$) or brushing teeth ($F = 3.929$, $p < .05$, partial $\eta^2 = .020$), turning off lights ($F = 4.103$, $p < .05$, $\eta^2 = .021$) and recycling batteries ($F = 4.542$, $p < .05$, partial $\eta^2 = .023$). In other cases, on the other hand, although participants in the experimental condition increased their willingness to adopt a sustainable target behavior (e.g. recycling glass, biking) more than participants in the control group, results are not statistically significant.

Table 7.1 Spillover

Item	$\Delta exp–\Delta cont$[1,2]	F	Significance[3]	Partial η^2
Biking to university	.22	.725		.004
Biking to shopping	.31	2.091		.011
Turning off lights when last person leaving a room	.20	4.103	*	.021
Turning off water while brushing teeth	.26	3.929	*	.020
Turning off water while soaping in the shower	.61	7.747	**	.039
Recycling paper	(.34)	.457		.005
Recycling glass	.07	1.681		.009
Recycling batteries	.37	4.542	*	.023
Car pooling	.08	0.48		.000

1 It represents the difference between the mean variations (before to post experiment) in experimental and control group participants (on a 1 to 7 scale). Positive values indicate that the willingness to uptake the specific green behavior increased more (decreased less) in the experimental group
2 negative numbers in brackets
3 *=significant at .05 level; **= significant at .01 level

The analysis hence confirms the spillover hypothesis, as participants encouraged to adopt a sustainable behavior (green purchasing) tend to be more willing to act consistently (that is, environment-friendly) also in other behavioral domains. At the same time, however, only easy-to-perform activities seem to be affected by the spillover phenomenon; simple curtailment behaviors such as turning off lights when the last person leaving a room, or turning off water while soaping in the shower, for instance. Whereas such behaviors are easy to adopt with little effort and no need to modify deeply rooted behavioral patterns, no spillover effect can be detected for more complex and costly behaviors like, for instance, transport mode. The results are consistent with prior research suggesting that spillover might be limited to *simple and painless* behaviors (Thøgersen & Crompton, 2009) that are easy to perform and that do not entail high financial costs or behavioral efforts.

Since data analysis is consistent with the spillover hypothesis (albeit limited to easy behaviors), research can move to the second step of the project, which analyzes whether the nature of incentives (RQ2) and habit strength (RQ3) have a role in affecting such positive propagation across behavioral domains. Let's first focus on incentives (monetary or praise rewards), and assess i) their direct impact on the behavior being incentivized and ii) their indirect impact on other, not-correlated behaviors. From this point on, only participants in the experimental conditions are considered for further analysis. Information contained in the shopping diaries was analyzed so as to shed light on the direct effect of monetary and non-monetary incentives on the purchase of green products. Table 7.2 illustrates the average number of items purchased by participants for each product category (numbers in brackets represent green products):

Table 7.2 Shopping diary – average number of (green) items purchased

	Monetary group		Praise group		Total	
Milk	8.57	(5.70)	6.18	(2.09)	7.55	(4.16)
Yoghurt	2.57	(1.39)	1.94	(0.68)	2.30	(1.09)
Eggs	2.09	(0.89)	1.94	(0.82)	2.03	(0.86)
Meat	6.33	(1.22)	4.88	(0.44)	5.71	(0.89)
Vegetables	12.52	(4.17)	10.18	(1.76)	11.53	(3.15)
Fruit	9.35	(2.52)	7.74	(1.26)	8.66	(1.99)
Detergents for house	1.09	(0.39)	0.65	(0.26)	0.90	(0.34)
Soap and personal hygiene products	2.02	(0.63)	1.59	(0.62)	1.84	(0.63)
Kitchen paper	0.35	(0.22)	0.35	(0.03)	0.35	(0.14)
Toilet paper	0.93	(0.50)	0.85	(0.24)	0.90	(0.39)

The results clearly show that monetary rewards are more effective in encouraging individuals to purchase green products. On average, participants in the praise group purchased 8.20 green products each, while participants in the monetary group 17.63. Also the relative share of green products in the total number of purchases varies significantly; indeed, organic food and eco-labeled products represent the 35.54 percent of total purchases for individuals in the monetary group, while the figure drops to 22.06 percent in the praise group. An ANOVA analysis was performed to assess the statistical significance of these preliminary results. In this new analysis, the independent variable is represented by the experimental groups (monetary or praise), whereas the percentage of organic and eco-labeled products over the total number of purchases represents the dependent variable. The difference in the percentage of green products purchased between the two groups is statistically significant ($F = 7.523$, $p < .01$, partial $\eta^2 = .088$), confirming that monetary incentives are more effective than verbal rewards, based on awareness and appraisal in encouraging people to adopt environmentally sound behaviors. Whereas this might come as little surprise, it is more intriguing to analyze whether the same pattern also features the *indirect* effect of incentives on behaviors; that is, are monetary rewards more effective also in triggering a positive spillover across behavioral domains? In order to answer this question, the study focuses on those target behaviors for which a positive spillover has been found by previous analyses, *turning off the light when the last person leaving a room*, *turning off the water while soaping in the shower or brushing teeth*, and *recycling batteries*. Table 7.3 shows descriptive statistics on the evolution over time (t_1 = pre-intervention to t_2 = post-intervention) in participants' intentions to perform the different behaviors.

In most cases, an increase in the intentions to adopt sustainable behaviors can be detected. At the same time, however, if we consider the differences between participants in the two groups, no clear pattern emerges: whereas for *turning off water while brushing teeth* and *recycling batteries* the monetary

Table 7.3 Monetary vs praise group

	Monetary group			Praise group		
	t_1	t_2	$\Delta t_2 - t_1$	t_1	t_2	$\Delta t_2 - t_1$
Turning off the light when the last person leaving a room	6.63	6.70	0.07	6.65	6.74	0.09
Turning off water while brushing teeth	6.46	6.59	0.13	6.74	6.71	−0.03
Turning off water while soaping in the shower	4.65	4.67	0.02	4.56	5.21	0.35
Recycling batteries	4.91	5.41	0.50	5.47	5.35	−0.12

Table 7.4 ANOVA results (rewards)

Item	$\Delta mon-\Delta pra^1$	F	p	Partial η^2
Turning off the light when the last person leaving a room	−.02	.081	.776	.001
Turning off water while brushing teeth	.16	.018	.894	.000
Turning off water while soaping in the shower	−.33	2.921	.091	.037
Recycling batteries	.62	1.397	.241	.018

1 Difference between the mean variations (pre- to post-experiment) in monetary and praise group participants (on a 1 to 7 scale). Positive values indicate how the willingness to take up the specific green behavior increased (positive) or decreased (negative) in the monetary group

group experiences stronger leaps in behavioral intentions, the opposite happens in the other target behaviors, *turning off the light when the last person leaving a room* and *turning off water while soaping in the shower*.

A one-way between-groups ANOVA was performed to test the statistical significance of these preliminary results, with the treatment group representing the independent variable and post-intervention scores for target behaviors representing the dependent variable. It is possible to control for the pre-intervention scores on the same target behaviors, representing this the covariate of the analysis whose results are presented in Table 7.4.

The emerging picture is controversial, as it is not possible to detect whether monetary or praise rewards are more effective in triggering a positive spillover. Furthermore, differences in changes of behavioral intentions between participants in the two experimental groups do not reach statistical significance – only the item "turning off water while soaping in the shower" shows marginally significant differences. The nature of incentives hence seems to have a strong direct impact on the behavior object of the inducement, yet no indirect impact on spillover trajectories can be detected.

The last aspect to be investigated refers to the role that habits play in shaping spillover trajectories. The additional data required to address the issue can be drawn from the habits section of the questionnaire, and specifically from questions adopting the Self-Reported Habit Index. Since an exceedingly long questionnaire would have affected the quality of responses, SRHI has been calculated for one target behavior only, recycling. Once again, notwithstanding complex and sophisticated statistical techniques could also be implemented to answer the specific research question on habits, I prefer to illustrate a simple, alternative methodology. This consists of dividing the sample (once again, only participants in the experimental condition are included in the analysis) in groups with different SRHI scores in the target behavior, and implement an ANOVA analysis to detect differences. Descriptive statistics on recycling SRHI scores and details about percentile cut-offs to be used in the analysis are illustrated in Table 7.5.

Participants could score 7 to 84 on the SRHI (a battery of 12 statements, with agreement expressed on a 1 to 7 scale). Information on percentiles shows that 10 percent of participants scored 16 or less, 20 percent of participants scored 31 or less, and so on. Three different analyses are performed. The first one compares participants that scored above and below the mean SRHI score of 51.5 (analysis 1: high vs low). The second analysis focuses on more *extreme* groups (that is, groups that diverge more significantly as far as the SRHI score is concerned) with participants belonging to the first and the last quintiles respectively (analysis 2: very high vs very low), while the last analysis focuses on participants in the first and last deciles (analysis 3: extremely high vs extremely low). In other words, subsequent analyses focus on groups of participants diverging more and more in terms of how habitudinal they are in the target domain of recycling. Table 7.6 illustrates the changes in recycling intentions over the six weeks of the experiment, with the general pattern suggesting that the increase is more apparent in participants with higher SRHI scores.

Table 7.5 Recycling SRHI

Mean	51.4571
Median	52
Standard deviation	21.387
Variance	457.404
Percentiles:	
10	16
20	31
50	52
80	73
90	78.4

Table 7.6 Intentions to recycle

Recycling SRHI		*Change in intentions to recycle*
High vs low	High	.32
	Low	.20
Very high vs very low	Very high	.40
	Very low	.05
Extremely high vs extremely low	Extremely high	.90
	Extremely low	(.30)

Table 7.7 ANOVA results (SRHI)

	F	p	Partial η^2
High vs low	.083	.16	.008
Very high vs very low	3.853	.057	.097
Extremely high vs extremely low	9.957	.006	.369

Individuals encouraged to purchase green products become more motivated to recycle the more habitual it is for them to perform such activity. In other words, the more they hold deeply rooted habits in recycling, the more an intervention in a different domain (green purchasing) makes them increase their willingness to recycle (that is, the stronger the spillover effect). Table 7.7 shows the ANOVA results, comparing groups scoring higher or lower on the recycling SRHI.

Results suggest that participants with deeply rooted habits in the domain of recycling experience stronger spillover effects, once exposed to the promotion of a different sustainable behavior like green purchasing. If we take a closer look at the numbers, we see that differences (and their statistical significance) increase the larger the difference on the SRHI score between groups. Whereas the difference is not statistically significant in analysis 1 ($F(1,103) = .803$, $p = .168$, partial $\eta^2 = .019$), and marginally significant in analysis 2 ($F(1,37) = 3.853$, $p=.057$, partial $\eta^2 = .097$), we notice that there is a highly significant difference between the "extremely high" and the "extremely low" groups ($F(1,18) = 9.957$, $p=.006$, partial $\eta^2 = .369$), which represent individuals that are respectively extremely habitual in recycling activities and not-habitual at all. Furthermore, the high partial η^2 in analysis 3 confirms that there is a very strong effect size – habit strength explains a large portion of the variance in the intention to recycle.

In conclusion, even a simple intervention study performed on a convenience sample of undergraduate students allowed light to be shed on crucial aspects of sustainable behaviors of citizens, and namely those that have been subject of previous chapters: habits, rewards and spillover. In brief, it has been possible to prove that there is indeed a positive spillover across behavioral domains, though this remains limited (at least in the short term) to easy activities that do not imply high behavioral or financial costs. Moreover, whereas monetary rewards seem to be more effective in encouraging the adoption of a specific behavior, it is more complex to assess whether the nature of rewards does affects also the strength of spillover. Habits, on the other hand, emerge as a construct that is indeed able to exert a strong effect on spillover trajectories.

Appendix: Online questionnaire

1. Preliminary information

1.1 Age:
1.2 Discipline you study at university:
1.3 Gender:
1.4 Student id number:
1.5 Are you usually responsible, at least partially, for the shopping in your household (yes/no)?
1.6 What is the approximate distance between your home and the university? (please tick the correct answer)
   – Less than 2 km
   – 2 km to 5 km
   – 5 km to 15 km
   – More than 15 km
1.7 Who do you live with? (please tick the correct answer)
   – With my parents
   – With my partner
   – Alone
   – I share an apartment with other students
   – Other
1.8 Are you a member of an environmental association? (please tick the correct answer)
   – Yes
   – No, and I have never been
   – No, but I have been in the past
1.9 For each of the following environmental issues, please state your concern using a 1 to 7 scale (1 = not concerned at all, 7 = very concerned):
   – Solid waste
   – Resource depletion
   – Air/water pollution
   – Chemical additives
   – Harm to nature
1.10 For each of the following statements on the relationship between humans and the environment, please state your agreement using a 1 to 7 scale (1 = I totally disagree; 7 = I totally agree):
   – We are approaching the limit of the number of people the earth can support.
   – Humans have the right to modify the natural environment to suit their needs.
   – When humans interfere with nature, it often produces disastrous consequences.

- Human ingenuity will insure that we do not make the earth unlivable.
- Humans are severely abusing the earth.
- The earth has plenty of natural resources if we just learn how to develop them.
- Plants and animals have as much right as humans to exist.
- The balance of nature is strong enough to cope with the impacts of modern industrial nations.
- Despite our special abilities, humans are still subject to the laws of nature.
- The so-called "ecological crisis" facing humankind has been greatly exaggerated.
- The earth is like a spaceship with very limited room and resources.
- Humans were meant to rule over the rest of nature.
- The balance of nature is very delicate and easily upset.
- Humans will eventually learn enough about how nature works to be able to control it.
- If things continue on their present course, we will soon experience a major environmental catastrophe.

2. Behavioral intentions

2.1   For each of the following behaviors, please answer using a 1 to 7 scale (1 = very unlikely, 7 = very likely) to the question *"How likely do you think you will do [X] in the next occasion, if you have the chance to do so?"* (where [X] stands for each behavior):
- Taking the bus or train to the university
- Taking the bus or train to shopping
- Biking to work
- Biking to shopping
- Turning off the light when you leave the room as last person
- Turning off the water when brushing your teeth
- Turning off the water while soaping in the shower
- Putting your paper waste in the recycle bin
- Putting your glass waste in the recycle bin
- Putting your plastic waste in the recycle bin
- Recycling exhausted batteries
- Printing your documents on both sides, to minimize paper use
- Reading documents on the computer instead of printing them, with the specific aim of minimizing paper use
- Buying organic food (vegetables, milk, meat)
- Buying shampoo, soaps or detergents with an eco-label

– Buying toilet paper or kitchen paper with an eco-label
– Minimizing the number of vehicles when you go out with friends using cars, considering as a driver to do so (besides economic savings, also the minimization of polluting emissions)

3. Pro-environmental behaviors

3.1 Please answer the following questions, according to a 1 to 7 scale (1 = never; 7 = always)
– Do you take the bus or train to the university?
– Do you take the bus or train to shopping?
– Do you bike to university?
– Do you bike to shopping?
– Do you turn off the light when you leave the room as last person?
– Do you turn off the water when brushing your teeth?
– Do you turn off the water while soaping in the shower?
– Do you put your paper waste in the recycle bin?
– Do you put your glass waste in the recycle bin?
– Do you put your plastic waste in the recycle bin?
– Do you recycle exhausted batteries?
– Do you print your documents on both sides, to minimize paper use?
– Do you read documents on the computer instead of printing them, with the specific aim of minimizing paper use?
– Do you buy organic food (vegetables, milk, meat)?
– Do you buy shampoo, soaps or detergents with an eco-label?
– Do you buy toilet paper or kitchen paper with an eco-label?
– When you go out with friends using cars, do you try to minimize the number of cars, considering as a driver to do so (besides economic savings, also the minimization of polluting emissions)?
3.2 Do you participate in green activism and volunteering (e.g. participating in public debates on environmental issues, actively supporting NGOs environmental awareness campaigns, organizing and participating to environmentalist demonstrations, cleaning up shores and river banks as part of environmental associations' campaigns, etc) ?
– I never have and I am not interested in doing it
– I never have but I would like to do it in the future
– I have done it once
– I do it occasionally (less than once a year)
– I do it regularly (each year)

3.3   Please state your agreement with each of the following statements, adopting a 1 to 7 scale (1 = I completely disagree, 7 = I completely agree)

 – I would support measures contributing to the reduction of greenhouse gases even if those measures meant paying more for fuel, electricity etc.
 – I would support policy measures aimed at protecting the environment and at reducing pollution, even if this might imply restrictions to citizens' behaviors in some environment-sensitive domains.

4. Habits and resistance to change

4.1   Please state your agreement with each of the following statements, on a 1 to 7 scale (1 = I totally disagree, 7 = I totally agree)

 – I generally consider changes to be a negative thing
 – I'll take a routine day over a day full of unexpected events any time
 – I like to do the same old things rather than try new and different ones
 – Whenever my life forms a stable routine, I look for ways to change it
 – I'd rather be bored than surprised
 – If I were to be informed that there-s going to be a significant change regarding the way things are done at work, I would probably feel stressed
 – When I am informed of a change of plans, I tense up a bit
 – When things don't go according to plans, it stresses me out
 – If my boss changed the criteria for evaluating employees, it would probably make me feel uncomfortable even if I thought I'd do just as well without having to do any extra work
 – Changing plans seems like a real hassle to me
 – Often, I feel a bit uncomfortable even about changes that may potentially improve my life
 – When someone pressures me to change something, I tend to resist even if I think the change may ultimately benefit me
 – I sometimes find myself avoiding changes that I know will be good for me
 – Once I've made plans, I'm not likely to change them
 – I often change my mind
 – Once I've come to a conclusion, I'm not likely to change my mind
 – I don't change my mind easily
 – My views are very consistent over time

4.2 Please state, for the following two behaviors, your agreement with each statement (on a scale 1 to 7: 1 = entirely disagree, 7 = entirely agree)
Buying organic food (vegetables, meat, milk) is something:
- I do frequently
- I do automatically
- I do without having to consciously remember
- That makes me feel weird if I do not do it
- I do without thinking
- That would require effort not to do it
- That belongs to my (daily, weekly, monthly) routine
- I start doing before I realize I'm doing it
- I would find hard not to do
- I have no need to think about doing
- that's typically "me"
- I have been doing for a long time

Recycling (glass, paper, plastic, batteries) is something:
- I do frequently
- I do automatically
- I do without having to consciously remember
- That makes me feel weird if I do not do it
- I do without thinking
- That would require effort not to do it
- That belongs to my (daily, weekly, monthly) routine
- I start doing before I realize I'm doing it
- I would find hard not to do
- I have no need to think about doing
- that's typically "me"
- I have been doing for a long time

Notes

1 This example is purely illustrative. The proposed partition of sustainable behaviors in the domains of modal choice, purchasing, recycling and curtailment is widely adopted in empirical investigations on the topic; yet, there are many other classifications in literature (e.g., Stern 2000).
2 Links to both versions were provided in the text of the email, as to encourage also international students to participate.
3 Around 300€ at the time of the study.
4 For reasons of space, only one line per product category is here reported.
5 For reasons of space, tables with the descriptive statistics of such preliminary results are not reported.
6 Behavioral intentions were chosen as the dependent variable, as given the short duration of the intervention sensible shifts in actual behaviors would have been extremely unlikely to be detected.

References

Dunlap, R. E., Van Liere, K. D., Mertig, A. G., & Jones, R. E. (2000). New trends in measuring environmental attitudes: measuring endorsement of the new ecological paradigm: a revised NEP scale. *Journal of Social Issues*, 56(3), 425–442.

Forbrugerstyrelsen og Miljøstyrelsen (1996). Miljøbelastningen ved familiens aktiviteter. Report 1996:1. Copenhagen: The National Consumer Agency.

Lanzini, P., & Thøgersen, J. (2014). Behavioural spillover in the environmental domain: an intervention study. *Journal of Environmental Psychology*, 40, 381–390.

Oreg, S. (2003). Resistance to change: Developing an individual differences measure. *Journal of Applied Psychology*, 88(4), 680.

Thøgersen, J., & Crompton, T. (2009). Simple and painless? The limitations of spillover in environmental campaigning. *Journal of Consumer Policy*, 32(2), 141–163.

Thøgersen, J., & Ölander, F. (2003). Spillover of environment-friendly consumer behaviour. *Journal of Environmental Psychology*, 23(3), 225–236.

Verplanken, B., & Orbell, S. (2003). Reflections on past behavior: A self-report index of habit strength. *Journal of Applied Social Psychology*, 33(6), 1313–1330.

Index

Note: page numbers in bold indicate illustations

 Taylor & Francis eBooks

Helping you to choose the right eBooks for your Library

Add Routledge titles to your library's digital collection today. Taylor and Francis ebooks contains over 50,000 titles in the Humanities, Social Sciences, Behavioural Sciences, Built Environment and Law.

Choose from a range of subject packages or create your own!

Benefits for you
>> Free MARC records
>> COUNTER-compliant usage statistics
>> Flexible purchase and pricing options
>> All titles DRM-free.

Benefits for your user
>> Off-site, anytime access via Athens or referring URL
>> Print or copy pages or chapters
>> Full content search
>> Bookmark, highlight and annotate text
>> Access to thousands of pages of quality research at the click of a button.

 REQUEST YOUR **FREE** INSTITUTIONAL TRIAL TODAY

Free Trials Available
We offer free trials to qualifying academic, corporate and government customers.

eCollections – Choose from over 30 subject eCollections, including:

Archaeology	Language Learning
Architecture	Law
Asian Studies	Literature
Business & Management	Media & Communication
Classical Studies	Middle East Studies
Construction	Music
Creative & Media Arts	Philosophy
Criminology & Criminal Justice	Planning
Economics	Politics
Education	Psychology & Mental Health
Energy	Religion
Engineering	Security
English Language & Linguistics	Social Work
Environment & Sustainability	Sociology
Geography	Sport
Health Studies	Theatre & Performance
History	Tourism, Hospitality & Events

For more information, pricing enquiries or to order a free trial, please contact your local sales team:
www.tandfebooks.com/page/sales

 Routledge
Taylor & Francis Group

The home of
Routledge books

www.tandfebooks.com

Printed in the United States
by Baker & Taylor Publisher Services